BUCKSHOT'S *Modern* TRAPPER'S GUIDE

For treme

Safety, Survival, Profit, Pleasure

By Bruce **"Buckshot"** *Hemming*

Quiet Wheel Books

Buckshot's *Modern* Trapper's Guide
For Xtreme Safety, Survival, Profit, Pleasure
By Bruce "Buckshot" Hemming

Published by: Quiet Wheel Books
PO Box 463180
Mt. Clemens, MI 48046

Distributed to the trade, specialty and consumer markets by:
QW, Inc
(800) 838-8854

Editorial Director: Rebecca J. Ensign
Cover Design and Technical Support: Blue Pencil Creative Group
Book Design: Michelle M. Ensign
Photos: Buckshot's Archives; georgesplace.com

Library of Congress Catalogue Card Number: 99-65154

10 9 8 7 6 5 4 3 2

184 pages; Soft Cover; ISBN 1-928547-00-1; $15.95

Dedication

I dedicate this book to my wife Linda who stood at the window for hours after dark waiting for my return from the wilds, wondering if I was alright. And who also spent days wading through my manuscript trying to catch all my grammatical errors before it was sent off to my Editor, Rebecca, so that this book could be understood by all trappers—the beginner and the veteran.

Acknowledgments

No man is an island and I'm no exception. Since I am not self-made, I would like to thank the people who have helped me through the years.

My father, Paul Hemming, who took the time to show me the great outdoors.

My cousin, Larry, who gave me my first box of muskrat traps, many years ago.

Charlie, who showed me how much fur I was missing.

Craig O'Gorman, who trained me and showed me the true meaning of a professional trapper.

Bill Knapp, who showed me the fine art of snaring.

The National Trappers Association who continues to stand up for what is right and has preserved the trapping tradition.

My many partners over the years who have shared the wonderful excitement of running traps together.

And to Craig Ring, the best partner I ever had.

Table of Contents

1

Scouting for Animals   3
Permission   11
Animal Tracks   15

2

Types of Traps   25
Modifying Your Traps   31
Preparing your traps   33

3

Water Trapping   41
Muskrats   44
Raccoons   48
Minks   51
Otters   53
Beavers   54

4

Land Trapping   61
Fox trapping   63
Coyotes   67
Bobcats   69
Raccoons, Opossums, and Skunks   71
Weasels   74
Fishers   75

5

Snaring   81
Snaring Beavers   86

6

Preparing the Animals   91

Fur Harvesters Pelt Handling for Profit   97

7

Tanning Fur   123

8

Eating Wild Game   129

9

Trapping Summer Pests and Nuisance Animals   145

10

Questions and Answers   151

A Word About Game Animals   163

When Animal Rights Become Animal Wrongs   167

Recommended Reading   173

About the Author   175

Scouting for Animals

In order to trap any animal you first have to find it. To do this, you must gain an understanding of its habits and habitat. For instance, muskrats live in marshes, ditches, ponds, and just about wherever there is water. Their main food is cattail roots, sweetflag, bulrush, apples, and if there is a cornfield near by their water source, they will eat corn, too. Muskrats are considered semi-aquatic animals, which means they breathe air and will spend some time out of the water, but most muskrat trapping is done in the water or underwater.

Raccoons, on the other hand, are found anywhere there is a good food source—farmers' fields, up in the oak groves, wild apple orchards, and along the water's edge. As another example, ground hogs dig big dens that can be seen for miles, making them very easy to trap. Just go look in the damp areas, the tracks will be there.

To find the animals, you'll first need to spend a lot of time in the area where you plan on trapping. The more time you spend in the woods, the better you will become at spotting signs. However, make sure you have basic know-how relative to the area where you will be scouting. For instance, when you are in bear country you must keep a clean camp. After eating your meal, clean up. Wash the dishes and burn the cans down so there is no smell from them. If you have fish, clean them in the river and make sure you throw everything in the water. Then mark your territory. I know this sounds funny, but it has always worked for me. When the call of nature comes, have everyone go around different sides of the camp and mark the area. Do all four sides. If you are going to be there for awhile, make sure you do this the whole time you are there. Bears are still afraid of humans and by doing this, even if the bear approaches the camp from the downwind side, he will get wind of one of the spots and leave. Of course, this is but one general rule for one particular situation. There is nothing like having a 12 gauge with slugs to help you sleep better at night.

Animals are just like humans. They take the easy way through an area to get to where they are going. Follow the trails and tracks you find to see why the animals are using them. Sometimes, you will see signs and tracks but won't be able to learn anything else. Well, in that case, as a friend of mine used to say, "When I don't know what is using the hole, I let a #220 solve the mystery."

You'll have the best success if you get out and walk the area you plan to trap. Farm roads after a rain, for example, will teach you a lot about what's in the area. So, after a rain, go walk a farm road. Wherever you have chosen, after walking it a couple times, note which way the wind is blowing. Does it consistently come from one direction? This is important if you plan on using bait or lure because the animal has to smell the bait or lure before you can catch him. Walk along the edge of the water. Look in the fresh mud. There should be tracks just about anywhere in America. I was recently walking the edge of a small trout stream and in less than ¼ mile I came across raccoon, mink, beaver, deer, and coyote tracks.

Just like us, all animals have to have food, water, and shelter. Their daily objective is to meet their needs. So, in order to understand the animal you want to trap you have to understand their needs and patterns. However, because animals' habits are never a fixed sequence, I must speak in general terms. So use the information in this chapter as guidelines only.

Some animals, like rabbits and squirrels, live their whole life within 1 square mile, whereas a tom bobcat may have a 50–75 mile hunting ground. Bobcats can take as long as three weeks to return to the area where you first saw their tracks. But, if the hunting is good for them in a particular area, they will stay around there for a few days.

If you want to trap mostly rabbits and squirrels, and it is legal in your state, you must learn where they live, what they are eating, and where they drink. Rabbits primarily eat grass, apples, garden vegetables, carrots, of course, and tree bark in the winter. Cottontail rabbits live in dens dug in the ground or in thick brush piles. With a couple of #110 Conibears, you can track cottontail rabbits to their den in the winter and trap them. Snowshoe hares (nicknamed "swamp rabbits") live their whole life in thick brush and always have a place where they duck under brush, just the perfect size for a #110. Jack rabbits live above ground but they may be able to be tracked to a place where the brush is all narrowed down.This shows you exactly where the rabbits are forced to travel. In that case, a #110 would take them. (A more detailed explanation of the Conibears is contained in Chapter 2–Types of Traps.)

Squirrels must have some type of nut source- oak, black walnut, hickory, beech, acorns, corn, etc. The five types of squirrels I know of are fox, black, gray, red, and flying squirrels. The fox squirrel is the largest and is most commonly seen in the city parks. The gray and black are just of a different color phase and can be born in the same litter. The red squirrels are the pesky, noisy ones that live everywhere in the woods. You'll also notice, when you're deer hunting, that they have big mouths. They won't hesitate to tell the world, from the tree they're in, that you are sitting directly below them. Squirrels are messy eaters and you will see the leftover crushed shells from their recent meals on stumps and fallen branches. All the large squirrels build nests of leaves and sticks that you see hanging in the tops of hardwood trees.

Don't overlook searching for animal droppings. The muskrat will have a toilet spot they use and you can easily find their droppings, each about ½ to 1 inch long, on a log, half in the water. Raccoons sometimes have a toilet spot on a stump or fallen tree. You will see several piles about 1 inch in diameter and 3-4 inches long. The coons' droppings are usually full of berry seeds. Fox, coyote and bobcat droppings look kind of like a dog's and you will find them on farm roads and logging trails. You will see tiny hair mixed in with their droppings. On occasion, I have seen fox droppings packed full of wild blackberry seeds. When looking for droppings in particular, take your dog along. He or she will stop at every one and mark them.

Once you decide what you want to trap, study a track guide such as the one included in this book so you can learn to identify the tracks when you see them. Then go out in your area and scout for the various signs. If you're just beginning, you won't go wrong by remembering that—*If there is water, there is fur.* For that reason, most people just getting started have the best success water trapping. The signs are easy to identify, and the trapping is easy and quick to learn. In addition, I recommend water trapping for survival. Game animals, such as squirrels and rabbits can be hunted down to nothing, as can deer and bears, however, you can't hunt muskrats out.

A friend of mine, when trapping a new area, used to save all his remains of bluegills after filleting. Then in early Fall, he would go to the area he planned to trap, dig a small hole and spread the dirt out in front of the hole. The bait was placed down in the hole and covered lightly with dirt. Then in two or three days he would come back and inspect for tracks. He said this really helped him, not only to identify what the animals were, but also to determine where to make sets. In the areas that didn't get action, he would ask himself, "Why did this bait station work and the next didn't?" He would always identify the pattern. As will you if you ask yourself why one thing worked and something else didn't. With traps in general, you can expect a 10% catch (1 catch per 10 traps set) per day on your dry land trapping. On your water trapping, you will go from 10 to 50% per day. See why most people prefer water trapping?

To scout for water animals, go to the area you have chosen for trapping and look for signs. Once you know what to look for, you will start seeing signs everywhere. A beaver, for example, usually has a trail that a blind man can find. That is because beavers go up on land to cut trees and their signs are everywhere—cut tree branches, trails, wood chips, etc.

Another example is the muskrat. Muskrats will have runways— little paths about four inches wide—through the seaweed. I can spot these from the highway at 65 mph. Muskrats also have what are called feed beds. A feed bed is an area where the muskrats will climb upon to eat. After they dive under the water to get their food, they will go back up to the surface and seek out a mound, or floating vegetation, and begin to eat their roots. You can spot these easily by looking for the bent down grass and peeled cattail roots. Muskrats live in under-water tunnels that they dig into the banks. In the fall, they build huts out of cattails and mud. A good rule of thumb is to count the muskrat huts and multiply that number by five. This will give you a rough estimate of the number of muskrats in a given area. You can safely trap three per hut every year. This will ensure you have muskrat meat and fur every year.

Back in the 70's, I knew of a trapper who didn't like marsh trapping. He noticed that right in the city along the roads, were little ditches with anywhere from 1 inch to over a foot of water. He used 150 #110 Conibears and in 30 days took over 1,000 muskrats. That was an average of 33 muskrats a day. Again, I have shared this to remind you that there are animals everywhere. You don't have to be in the wilderness to catch large numbers. In fact, studies have shown the best place to trap is in active farm country.

In general, farmland will have coons, foxes, coyotes, opossums, and ground hogs. Mountain terrain has small streams, rivers and lakes. There you will find minks, coons, beavers, otters, muskrats, some coyotes and bobcats. Wilderness areas, like the great Smoky Mountains up though Maine, contain about the same types of animals. Out in the Southwest, you will find gray foxes, coyotes, bobcats, and some coons.

Foxes and coyotes in farm country can sometimes be hard to detect. I have trapped farms where I didn't see one track and just set up on what I felt would be the animals' hunting patterns and took fox. Tracks and signs are just indicators, they tell you where to set and what to set for, but they do not tell the whole story. The traps tell the story. Case in point: I have set traps on smoking, hot, fresh coon tracks and in a week never caught a coon. Why? Because the coons found something better to eat than what the water was offering.

Nevertheless, don't let that example stop you from *setting on Signs.* If you scout the area you have chosen several times in advance of setting your traps, you'll get a feel for the land and develop an instinct for knowing where to look.

A Scouting Tale from the Bush

I recently floated a river scouting for fur. My cousin Larry was with me. Together, we learned a great deal more about nature, animals, camping and fishing. There is nothing better in the world than being out with someone who appreciates the great outdoors and is always eager to learn. You'll find that both of you will want to try and learn new things to make the experience even more enjoyable.

I was looking for fresh muskrat droppings on open logs in the sun so I could get a clear picture of the signs. The first thing I noticed was the effect the current had on the muskrat sign. The faster the current, the more the muskrat would avoid it—even though there was good food around. I realized that, to the muskrat, fighting the current was not worth the energy needed to obtain the food.

I did spot some logs in the clearing, but they had only a few droppings on them. It seemed the preferred logs were those that had both ends out of the water, with the middle immersed. These made excellent feed beds as they were able to float in between this dip and feed and rest on either side of the log.

After two days of floating, I discovered the best sign for the muskrat—they need overhead cover. I learned to look for a slow moving current with grass and roots overhanging in the water. The best log sign turned out to be a small log, 3 inches in diameter, paralleling the shoreline with a pine tree directly above it. On this little log, the muskrats had several piles of droppings; as many as fifteen in various stages of freshness. I reasoned then, that the area had a high owl population and the muskrats soon learned to feed under cover before the silent deadly predator from above swooped down and ruined their night. Again, this shows that once you begin thinking like the animal you are scouting, you will start to know where to look for signs. Once you get the hang of it, you will quickly discover more signs.

I observed that beavers also prefer the slower current. They prefer to set up bank dens up to ½ mile up and down from the rapids. There was rarely more than one den. But, I concluded that this was related more to the available food supply than anything else. Sometimes their den would be in the slow current just before rapids so I swung the canoe down beside any log that stuck out from the shore one to two feet and paralleled the river. By looking carefully, I could make out the trail of the beaver swimming beside the log, made when its back feet scraped the bottom. I noticed also that they left several trails where they had climbed out of the bank of the river in search of food. If you ever discover this scenario, it is a good set location for a #330 Conibear.

From paying close attention, I discovered two consistent fur sign areas: logs strewn across the river (they will almost always have some faint claw marks from the animals that use them as bridges) and every side drainage, creek or run off with water. (You can safely consider these signs fur magnets.) Every drainage with water had beaver, muskrat, coon, and sometimes mink sign, and occasionally a beaver dam. A coon trail was always over that first dam and occasionally I could make out a bobcat trail. It appeared that the animals that hunted the area soon learned where the beaver dams were, as coon and mink have learned to hunt dams for fish, crawfish, and frogs.

Each time you go out, you will learn something new. From that one trip, I gained many lessons. Among them:

1. Always set the small waterways flowing into the main river.
2. Look for cover that will protect the muskrat.
3. Look for crossings over the river to take advantage of easy sets.
4. Think like a predator and ask, what is the easiest way to hunt and cross this river?
5. Bring a notebook along to document how many and what types of traps will be needed.
6. On the scouting trip, set up little sticks and logs in the trails so the animals will get used to walking or swimming through certain narrowed down spots.

In general, the most important thing you can do is get out there and get a feel for nature and the lay of the land. As mentioned earlier, make sure you understand the composition of the area—watch out for snakes, poison ivy, bears and such. But, overall, have fun. Take the kids. The energy of youth is boundless and there is no better quality time in the world than being in the woods with your kids sharing this experience. Teach them to look for sign. Believe me, after a while they will start finding more sign than you.

Permission

Most of the best trapping is done on active farms. I'm not talking hobby farms but the actual farms with cows, corn, wheat, and rye fields. The active farms have food, shelter and water for the animals. Most have hedgerows, which is always good for trapping. The farmers will love the trapper who takes out the problem critters, like ground hogs, badgers, raccoons, muskrats, and beaver. So you already have an advantage approaching the farm. The disadvantages you face are previous hunters and trappers who didn't respect the farmer's property and were careless.

When you approach the farm, the best time is Saturday afternoon, just go up and ask permission to trap whatever you plan to trap. Say for instance, as you approach you see a stream dammed up from beaver. That is what you ask to trap first. If you see a small pond, ask to trap muskrats. If you see groundhogs ask the farmer if he is having trouble with ground hog holes. The whole idea is to show the farmer the advantage to allowing you on the property.

You want to make sure you are clean, shaved and wearing clean clothes. In short, you should look like someone who is responsible. The farmer may have had hunters come in and shoot toward the house or left gates open and caused the farmer more work from their neglect. So you have to be responsible. Let the farmer know that it is his property and you will respect his wishes. If he wants you to walk the farm, then walk. If he doesn't want you to shoot, then don't. Tell him you will use Conibears only. If there are cows, ask where the cows are going to be and make sure you close every gate behind you.

The best way in my area is to ask permission to trap raccoons. The raccoons like to get into barns and tear things up and the farmers get tired of cleaning up after them. In addition, coons can and do tear up huge sections of corn. Every bushel of corn the coons get, is one less that the farmer gets. I guarantee if there is corn, there are coons. Coons are easy to trap and if you are farm trapping, you will quickly earn back your investment for your traps.

The farmer will ask you questions like, how long have you been trapping? Don't lie. If it is your first year then tell him that. Take your kids along and if you plan on taking them with you, let the farmer know you are trying to teach your kids how to trap. You want to teach your children responsibility and you intend to get them away from TV and Video games. This is your goal. Be friendly, most farmers are just hard working Americans who are doing their best to make a living. So your approach should always be a friendly, "you're the boss, it's your farm, you set the rules and I will follow them."

If you're down south I hear there is a major beaver problem. You cannot only ask farmers for permission, but you can also check with the big logging companies, Christmas tree farms, or any private property the beaver are tearing up. Remember your job is to find places to trap. Check with your state DNR or Fish and Wildlife Division and ask if there are any complaints from local farmers or property owners. You are providing a service. This is how I deal with off-season problem animal complaints. If I hear about someone who has a beaver problem I contact that person and go out and take a look at the property.

If it is a good working farm where I know I can catch other fur bearers in the fall, I will trap the one or two problem beavers or raccoons for permission to trap that fall. If the place is not that good for fall trapping then I charge $25-$35 per animal. This is the going rate and most people gladly pay it. So you can trap beaver in certain areas and make quite a living doing it. But that is on huge tracts of land own by timber companies. They will expect results and will not keep you around unless you are going to produce.

The Delta Waterfowl study mentioned earlier involved hiring a trapper to trap all the predators in Towner County, North Dakota around the ducks' nesting area. The trapper was very good and was nailing the predators as fast as they appeared. Guess what the study proved? In the area where the predators were reduced by trapping, 71% of all ducklings hatched, and survived to fly south. In the area where the predators were not reduced, 150 nests were found and only 21 hatched. This study proved beyond a shadow of a doubt the value of trapping. It makes me laugh at times how people can't see the pure purpose of trapping. The value of trapping is in helping the land stay within the carrying capacity limits so all animals can flourish.

But, since I don't have a Ph.D. after my name, I can't possibly know what I'm talking about, right? Wrong! When I heard an "expert" ask "Why are the song bird populations falling in numbers?" I laughed. I have been writing for years on the value of trapping and the relationship of predator and prey while the "experts" scratch their heads. The "experts" never learned the rule of carrying capacity of the land and how everything must stay in balance for nature to work. Wildlife advocates who say nature will take care of itself forget one tiny little fact. Ever since the first cave man picked up a club and killed his first animal, man became a part of nature. And man always will be part of nature and that is what God intends us to be.

I got a little off track but the point I'm making is to never worry about the morality of trapping. When you approach someone to ask for permission to trap, know that you are doing right. Some farmers will say no, but others will love having you there and if you treat their property with respect, you will be invited back year after year.

Life is simple. People make it complicated. So, treat others the way you would want someone to treat you and your property. Be polite and courteous, if the farmer's fence is down and the cows are running loose, stop in and let the farmer know. If I see a fence knocked over, I will set it back up and stop and tell the farmer where the break is. If I see someone tearing up the fields I'll stop them and ask what they're doing there.

If you make a great catch on the farm, stop and show the farmer and thank him for allowing you on the farm. When you are finished trapping, make sure you stop in and say "thank you for allowing me on your property, this is what I caught, and if it's OK, I'll be back next year." Common courtesy goes a long way. One other thing you should know—it is best not to bother the farmers on Sunday. This is their day of rest and you are disturbing them. Some don't care but others are touchy on the subject, so simply respect their wishes.

The big thing to remember is, ask the farmer what the rules are. Let him/her know what time you will be on the farm. Find out if it's OK to shoot small game when you're checking traps. Ask if there are going to be any hunters on the farm. Find out if you can drive to the back 40. Ask if you should walk back if it is raining. Ask about their pets and how close to the house you should set the nearest trap.

The most important question to ask is "where are the fur bearers?" The farmer has a good idea where the coons are coming from, which corner the fox is entering the fields, where the beaver lives and how many muskrats are in the pond. There is a wealth of information he can tell you, but only if you ask will you hear the answer.

Remember you are representing all trappers, so if you do wrong, the whole world will hear about it. Be courteous, treat the property with respect, and stop and let the farmer know all the good things. I trap on 15 farms in the fall, sometimes up to 20, but generally around 15 and I have been doing it for years on the same ones just because I do what the farmers want and help them out when I can. I trap ground hogs for them, not because I can sell the fur, but to help build a relationship with the farmer.

Last thing to remember, if you want to trap a lot of farms, seek out the farmer who is having trouble with animals. If someone else beats you to a farm and permission has already been granted, skip that farm and go to the next. Just starting out, you are not going to beat an experienced trapper, so why go through the heartache? Simply move onto the next farm. If you plan on being a hobby trapper and only run 12 traps, then one or two farms are all you need. Some hobby trappers set on Friday afternoon, check Saturday, and pull the traps on Sunday. Whatever you want to do just go out and have fun. You are not going to make a pile of money trapping but there is absolutely no reason you can't pay for your equipment the first year, meet a lot of good people and have fun.

Animal Tracks

Tracks are one of the telltale clues for detecting the presence of wild animals. Tracks are your evidence as to the activity, abundance, range and habits of a particular animal. By learning to recognize and distinguish animal tracks, you can begin documenting an animal's behavior and whereabouts. As outlined below, there are many dimensions to tracks.

Footprints

Each animal has a unique footprint. The size, shape and pattern can help you identify who or what passed through. Look for tracks in snow, sand, and mud, especially next to water sources such as a streambed or lakeside. Wait a couple of days after a rain and go check the mud puddles and low areas for tracks.

The number of toes can tell you a lot about a track. Many animals have a different number of toes on their forefeet and hind feet. As these animals bounce along, they often leave tracks with their hind feet ahead of their forefeet. Rabbits, when running, will do this.

Skunks, muskrats, opossums (or possums) and raccoons have feet with five toes. These animals, among others, leave both heel and toe impressions on the ground.

Coyotes, bobcats, and foxes have four toes to all their feet. These animals only leave tracks with their toes and pads.

Elk, deer, antelope, sheep, and cows walk on specialized toenails called hooves. Look for the spilt halves. It is an old wives' tale that you can tell a buck deer if you see the dew claws in the print. The dew claws are two small bumps that look like the bottom of a dog paw. They are about two inches up from the hooves.

Bird tracks have three or four finger like markings. Game birds, quail, dove and some ducks walk along as they feed, leaving alternating tracks. Perching birds like robins and sparrows hop around leaving side by side or paired tracks. Birds often leave both tail and wing marks when taking off in flight. If you have ever seen ruffled grouse or pheasant tracks in the snow you know what to look for.

Members of the dog family leave claw marks in their tracks. Coyotes and foxes tend to move in a straight line where dogs like to wander from side to side. Dogs have the luxury of a constant food supply. Fox and coyotes have to earn their food every day so they tend not to waste anytime.

Members of the cat family can retract their claws and seldom leave claw marks in their tracks. If you know what housecat tracks look like, just imagine a cat twice that size and you know what bobcat tracks look like.

Muskrats leave curving tail markings between their prints. You will see the prints and a tail drag mark. Beavers also drag their tails, especially in snow. Beavers, like ducks and gulls, have web feet to help them swim.

Distance

Distance is the spacing between a set of tracks and will often indicate if the animal was walking or running. Follow the tracks and see if the distance changes. A bobcat has about a 10 inch spacing between each track while walking in open ground. When at a full run, its prints can be spaced 4 to 8 feet apart. You read that right. A bobcat can indeed have an 8 foot spread in between track prints.

Patterns

Members of the dog and cat family as well as hoofed animals walk in a straight line. Cats often walk so straight that their back foot lands in the front foot print.

Skunks and porcupines more or less waddle along, usually searching for plants or grubs to feed on.

Snakes and insects also leave tracks when they move over sand or wet soil. The snake will leave curved lines. Insects leave very fine tracks often in two rows.

Wild animals mark their territory in different ways. Foxes, coyotes and bobcats tend to use a urine post to mark their area. Just like dogs, the other animals will approach and mark in the same place. This will result in fights when the two meet.

Beavers and muskrats have special glands for marking their territory. The beaver gland is called a castor gland. This is used to make lure. Beavers are vicious fighters and when they become over crowded, you will catch beavers with scarred tails and large bite marks through the pelts. Muskrats have a musk gland and are the same as beaver, fighting over territory and females. The males will be scarred up. With trapping, you can keep the population at normal levels and slow this down.

All animals have their own way of marking their little kingdom. The cycle of life is funny. A red fox can be the top predator until the coyote moves in taking the area over by force. The coyote can be top predator until the wolf moves in and takes the area by force. The rule of the wild always hold true, you are either predator or prey. Even if you are a predator, you can become prey to a larger predator.

I remember one year I pre-baited an area for foxes and had foxes all over my sets in just one section of woods. I was thinking I would easily take five red foxes off that one section. Do you know how many I took? None! A wolf moved into the area and the fox quickly left for safer grounds. This is just one example of how a smaller predator can become prey.

Do you know why coons like to stay near brush and trees? Coyotes. The coon is a predator to frogs and fish, but becomes prey to the coyote. That is the cycle of life and man is a part of this cycle.

For more specific information on animal tracks and signs, refer to **Animal Tracks and Signs of North America** by Richard P. Smith which contains actual photos of animal and bird tracks as they appear in the wild. The book sells for $16.95 and is available through QW, Inc (800) 838-8854. Mention that you heard about it in this book and you will receive a "Buckshot discount."

The following pages illustrate the tracks of the most frequently trapped animals. Bear in mind, these illustrations are much more detailed than you will find in natural conditions.

Coyote Tracks

Gray Fox Tracks

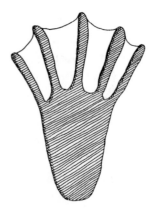

Beaver Tracks

Illustrations by Kim A. Cabrera; www.geocities.com/Yosemite/Rapids/7076/

Red Fox Tracks

Mink Tracks

Otter Tracks

Illustrations by Kim A. Cabrera; www.geocities.com/Yosemite/Rapids/7076/

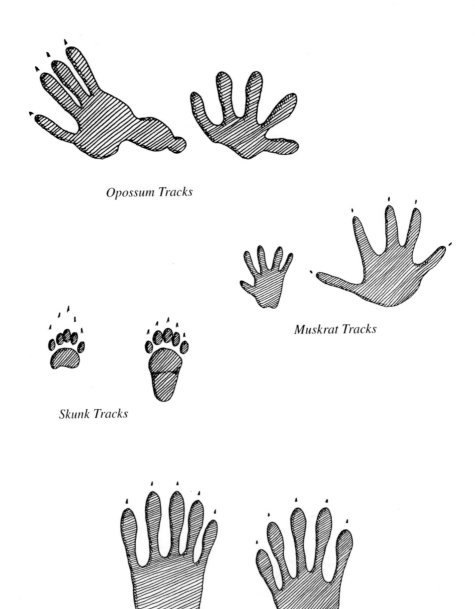

Opossum Tracks

Muskrat Tracks

Skunk Tracks

Raccoon Tracks

Illustrations by Kim A. Cabrera; www.geocities.com/Yosemite/Rapids/7076/

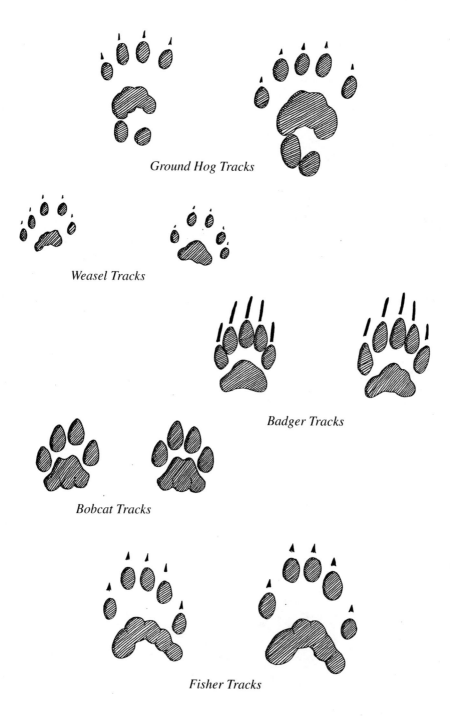

Ground Hog Tracks

Weasel Tracks

Badger Tracks

Bobcat Tracks

Fisher Tracks

Illustrations by Kim A. Cabrera; www.geocities.com/Yosemite/Rapids/7076/

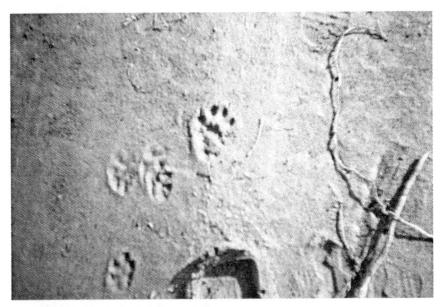

Bobcat tracks made by 2 different bobcats.

Active beaver hut; notice the fresh cutting at the far right of hut.

Hollow log; This is a coon, mink and muskrat magnet.

A fresh beaver cutting.

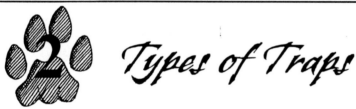

Types of Traps

raps have existed as long as trapping has. And, as man has advanced, so have the traps. Over the years, here in America, trap manufacturers, such as Blake and Lamb, Onieda, Northwoods, Montgomery, and others, have come and gone. The objective of this chapter is to familiarize you with the most prevalent traps, names and types.

Trap types are abbreviated. For example, L.S stands for long-spring, C.S. stands for coil-spring, #2–4 coil O.S. is a #2 four coil with offset jaws. There are many more and different traps out there, old and new. I don't intend to cover them all. That would just confuse the issue. We will cover the single long-spring, double long-spring, coil-spring, 4 coil-springs, body gripper, cage traps, and in a separate chapter, snares.

One concept and term you should know, although I don't get into it, is stoploss. This is related to the single long-spring, which is for muskrat trapping, and all it means is that a spring-loaded arm, after the jaws close, rides up the animals leg. Again, I don't care for them because you have to adjust them all the time and if you use #1½ long-springs in deep water, the muskrat will be drowned shortly. For the shallow water, where you can't drown the muskrat, use the #110 Conibears. This is my opinion. If you like the stoploss, then by all means use them.

I have used traps from all of the companies and have my preferences. Ultimately, I recommend that you use whatever you have found, or do find, you like best. I personally use BMI, Bridger and Duke, which along with Victor, are the leading companies. I also have some old Northwoods #1¾ that I modified and they will stay with me.

There is an emergence right now of small new trap companies who are building specialized traps, like the MB-750 leg-hold, which was designed by a trapper to correct the problems (thin jaws, for example) associated with leg-holds manufactured by the large trap companies. The trap was designed for beaver and retails for $28.00 each. While Victor is still around, I personally won't own one because, in my opinion, the company sold out the trappers in California in the late '70s and early '80s. Victor advocated the outlawing of all steel traps, except the rubber jaw traps. At the time, Victor had the only rubber jaw trap; thus, they cornered the market through legislation. Apparently, not enough people knew that the tests performed on live animals have proven that off-set jaws are more humane than even rubber jaw traps.

Most people have preconceived ideas about the humanity of traps. I know I did until I started trapping, then I realized that much of what is publicized are half-truths. The trap, if used properly, is quite humane and becomes only a restraining devise. Furthermore, the pain induced by a leg-hold going off on your hand is far less than the pain from being in handcuffs. (I know. I worked in law enforcement and have been placed, and have placed people, in handcuffs.)

Single Long-Spring Traps (Leg-holds)

The single long-spring traps (abbreviated L.S.) today come in only two sizes #1 and #1½. The #1 is the most popular. Most people who have trapped muskrats may remember using them. The jaw spread is 4 inches when open. The #1 can be used for muskrats, rabbits, squirrels, and weasels. The #1½ is the same thing, only larger and is used for water trapping the four animals mentioned above. It's a little weak for land trapping. Because of its larger size and 4¾ inch jaw spread, the #1½ trap will hold coons and mink that may get caught in your muskrat trap. In addition, its added weight aids in drowning the muskrat quicker.

Here's an old trick for adding more weight to the #1. Take some trap wire, bend it over to form an arch in a dixie cup. The top of the arch should be about three inches high from the rim of the dixie cup. Fill the cup with cement. Once dried, attached it by the wire to the trap. Once caught, the muskrat dives for deep water and the extra weight takes him to the bottom.

With most leg-holds, or long-spring traps, there is what is called a pan, a dog and a tension jaw. The dog (the lever that flips over and holds the trap open by hooking into the trigger) is placed over the tension jaw and under the pan notch. Then you lower the pan so it goes off easy when the animal steps on the pan.

Double Long-Spring Traps

Double long-springs have been around for years. This is the trap the early Mountain Men used. Today, these traps come in the following sizes:

#11   A double spring #1
#2   Good for land tapping fox and coons
#3   Used for land trapping coyotes and some beaver
#4   Beaver traps
#5   Beaver traps, although you could catch and hold a mountain lion or wolf

Coil-spring Traps

Coil-spring traps (abbreviated C.S.) are very popular. They are my main choice for land trapping. Because they are lighter in weight, you are to be able to carry more of them. They come in #1, #1½, #1¾, #2, and #3. I don't care for the #1 Coil-spring, it's alright as a water trap, but I would prefer to have a #1½ long-spring.

The #1½ Coil-spring is a great trap for southern trappers and early season Northern trappers who don't have a lot of snow. This trap has caught thousands of foxes, raccoons and minks and is one very popular trap. The only downside to them that I have found is that the big northern coon can power out of them. I have had coyotes pull the jaws right out of the traps. Because of that, I switched to the #1¾.

The 4 coil traps are very good because of their life span. The average life on a #2 coil is about three years. At that point, the springs need to be replaced. The 4 coil-spring traps, on the other hand, can last for years. Some of mine are five years old (as of this writing) and are still working great.

BMI sells a #1¾ professional 4 coil for large animals like coyotes and large coons and I have had a lot of success with them. BMI made the jaws almost a full ½ inch across. With the offset model and a little modifying you have a top-notch trap. The #2's are about the same and are for coyotes and winter trapping where there isn't too much snow. The #3 coil-spring is the standard for catching coyotes but I have caught beaver in them. I have been very pleased with the results of the Bridger #3 offset.

Conibear Traps

Named after its inventor, Frank Conibear, who sold the rights in 1958, the Conibear is also called the body gripper. It is considered one of the most humane traps because it kills most animals within a few minutes. One study in Canada found the average beaver dies within four minutes of being caught. I have watched many muskrats get caught. In less than a minute, they were dead. The only bad part about Conibears is that if you catch a dog or a cat, it is dead, so you must be very careful where you set these traps.

With a leg-hold, you can let the pets go. Their feet will be sore for a few days, but they will recover.

The trap comes in the following sizes, although the three most common are the #110, #220 and #330.

#110 single spring 4½ inch by 4½ inch.
Mostly used for muskrats, but is a good mink, rabbit, and squirrel trap and, in an emergency, can be used for duck, pheasant, quail, fish and small blackbirds.I like the #110.

#120
The same trap as the #110, but with two springs. Designed for mink and marten trapping.

#160
(This size through the #330 are double springs and you need a setting tool for them.) This trap is 6 inches by 6 inches and was designed for ground hogs and smaller coons. I don't care for this trap. I have had coons jump over this trap when set on trails.

#220
A double spring, 7 inches by 7 inches; my preferred trap for coons, possums, and ground hogs but is also used for skunks and, in an emergency, can be used for geese, fish and other similar size animals.

#280
This trap is 8 inches by 8 inches and is one powerful trap. I have caught beaver and otter in them. However, I have had beaver swim up to them and turn around because the opening was not large enough, so I don't use these any more.

#330
This trap is 10 inches by 10 inches and is my favorite beaver trap. It is a double spring designed for beaver, otter, and bobcats but in an emergency can be used for feral dogs, geese, fish over 30 pounds and other similar size animals.

Cage or Live Traps

The cage trap or live trap is acceptable. If you have a garden to protect, you can catch the animal, take the trap with the animal in it and take them for a drive to relocate them. This trap is good on farms that have pets. If the pet gets caught, it can be released unharmed. You can use the live trap for raccoons in the barn, but they are not practical for any serious trapping because of their bulk, weight, and expense, $40-$50 each.

Essential Traps

If I were trapping for survival, I would have the following: 4 dozen medium size snares for beaver, fox, coyote, 4 dozen small snares for rabbits and squirrels, 3 dozen special cam loc snares strong enough to hold deer, six #110 Conibears for small animals, four #220 Conibears for medium animals like raccoon, two #330 Conibears for beaver, and four #1 ½ coil springs.

With that in mind, I highly recommend you buy the Survivor pack. Designed as a complete package, it will provide survival trappers as well as beginners with the best possible "arsenal." Each kit comes with the following items.

1 dozen small game snares
1 dozen medium size snares
6 #110 Conibear
4 #220 Conibear
2 #330 Conibear
1 setting tool
4 1½ coil-springs
Logwood dye (to blacken the traps and to remove all smell)
3 bottles of lure—one each for muskrat, beaver and raccoon
One roll of wire for tying off the traps
Video #1–"Survival Trapping" which explains trap parts, different traps, lures, 10 different sets, complete skinning, fleshing, and stretching of a raccoon and where to sell your fur for profit.
Video #2–"10 Homemade Traps" to show how you can build foolproof traps out of common household items.
1 copy (comes autographed) of "Buckshot's Modern Trapper's Guide..."

The whole kit is only $229.95 and can be ordered by phoning (906) 482-2831. A small price to pay for a guaranteed return of five rabbits for the stew pot, ten beaver pelts for staying warm and protection of your garden and livestock.

Modifying Your Traps

As mentioned earlier, the traps you have, with a little modification, can be made into top-notch traps. Following is one way to modify a trap.

To devise this method, tests were performed using leg-hold traps. The one that produced the best results and proved to be the most humane to the animals was one that had thicker jaws, offset jaws, 3 swivels, and a shock absorber in-line spring. Again, each of these features was designed with the animal's comfort in mind.

Thicker jaws. Some trappers do what is called laminating which means adding to the jaw thickness to displace the energy of the springs. This is done by welding on #9 wire or ¼ inch round stock, or ³⁄₁₆ inch flat stock, to the top of the jaws.

The thicker jaws displace the spring energy onto a larger area and, with the offset jaws, the trap becomes only a restraining device. The easiest way to demonstrate the effect of this feature is by asking you if you have ever pinched your fingers with needle nose pliers? If so, have you ever pinched your fingers with regular pliers with the same amount of pressure? Which hurt more? The needle nose pliers, of course! Basically, they penetrate a smaller surface so they break the skin quicker and penetrate deeper.

Offset jaws. With the jaws offset ¼ inch, blood will still flow down through the paw. The old style trap closes tight, which makes the animal's foot go numb and causes the animal to fight the trap more.

3 swivels. The swivels are based upon the idea that the animal circles the stake and rolls on the ground. With the swivels, the animal is unable to kink the chain up, which could result in a sprained or broken leg. The swivels stop that from happening, again more animal comfort in mind.

Shock absorber spring. This was designed to work just like a shock absorber on your car. As the animal fights the trap, he pulls on the chain to the stake (referred to as "in-line.") In-line spring stretching reduces shock on his paw and tires the animals out quicker. Tests

31

have shown that once caught in the trap, an animal will have an accelerated heartbeat and an increase in adrenaline for around the first 15 minutes, then he relaxes. At just before first light, when most animals are heading back to sleep all day, the trapped animal again fights the trap for around 15 minutes. After that, he will lie down and go to sleep and his heartbeat and adrenaline almost returns to normal.

Essentially, unmodified older traps are not as productive. You will catch more animals if you modify your traps to the above standards. Simply put, modified traps equal more animals caught and more food for the table. If you are going to depend on your traps for survival, then use the best.

A perfect example is that after I modified my traps, my pull out rates for raccoons dropped from 20% to 5%. You see, raccoons are very powerful animals. They will stand on the trap, pull their feet out, then run back home. I'm sure they end up with sore feet for a couple of days, but I know they survive because I have had trap-smart raccoons set off my traps without getting caught. This situation, repeatedly observed over the years, prompted me to devise my trap tricks. The smart coons I have caught with my modified traps are all healthy with no paw damage from their previous encounter with the trap.

"Simply put, modified traps equal more animals caught and more food on the table."

Jaw spread—The Size of the Span of the Trap's Jaws

Size/Type	Jaw spread	Used For
#1 L.S.	4 inches	Muskrat,weasel (rabbit size)
#1½ L.S	4¾ inches	Muskrat (smaller coon size)
#1½ C.S.	4⅞ inches	Fox, raccoon (groundhog size)
#1¾ C.S.	5¼ inches	Fox, raccoon (coyote size)
#2 C.S.	5½ inches	Light snow fox (coyote size)
#3 C.S.	6¼ inches	Coyote, bobcat (beaver size)
#2 D.L.S.	5 inches	Fox, raccoon (opossum size)
#3 D.L.S	6 inches	Coyote, beaver (bobcat size)
#4 D.L.S.	6½ inches	Beaver (coyote size)
#5 D.L.S.	7¼ inches	Beaver, mountain lion (wolf size)

You will notice that some animals can be caught in different size traps. There are many reasons for this, the most common being different conditions, weather and animal size. The more experience you gain and the more attention you pay to the variances in your catches, the easier it will be for you to learn what trap to use, when, where and why.

Preparing your traps

Preparing your traps is the very important first step to success. So make sure you do it right. The time spent adjusting, dyeing, painting and making them look good and work well is the key to productive trapping. Why go through all the trouble of trapping if you are going to have animals refuse to go into your trap?

I know of some trappers who only rust their traps and then wonder why I catch more animals than they do. Just like life, it is the small details that make the difference. If there is a critter that walks, flies, or swims, you can catch it. It doesn't matter what they are. So, if you are lazy in the preparation phase, you will pay later.

Adjusting Your Traps

If the Conibear traps are new, they can be really powerful so you may want to leave the safety catches on for a month to weaken them up. Doing this will ensure that they are easy to handle. If you're strong enough or comfortable enough with the traps, skip this part. When you first get the traps, you have to adjust them, check them out, test them, and make sure all is in working order. On Conibears, this is simple. All you do is set them and fire them on a stick. Check to see that the trigger works properly and that the trap closes fast and tight on the stick.

On the #110, you can just wire them open and leave them set for a week or two, whatever length of time makes you feel most comfortable. If all goes well, meaning you can set the trap with ease, then you de-grease, rust, and speed dip in black.

The leg-holds are a different story. There are a lot of things to do. First, you must set and test fire. The next step, adjusting the pan level, is one of the most important. You want the pan level with the top of the set jaw. If the top is too high, then bend the dog arm in to bring the pan down. If the pan is too low, then bend it out to raise the pan.

Once you get the pan level, the next step is to file the dog and pan notch flat. The traps come from the factory with a little roughness. You want that gone so when the animal steps on the trap it goes off crisp and smooth with no creeping downward. The trap should feel similar to a good rifle with a crisp snap as you squeeze the trigger. Use a stick to feel this, or lift up the loose jaw and, under the jaws, push the pan down to get the feel. This should allow the trap to fire without your hand getting caught.

For coil-spring traps, if the pan has any side wobble, you may have to take out the nut and bolt that holds the pan on. Add one or two washers to the inside to make everything even and smooth. You can bend the opening a little to add the washers—again, just make sure everything is even and smooth. You can also adjust the pan pressure so that it only fires at a certain poundage to ensure you trap the animal you set out to trap. However, I have purchased used traps that didn't fire until they had 6 lbs. of pressure. If you want to go after the foxes and coyotes, then adjust to 2 lbs. I adjust my fox traps to 2 pounds to keep rabbits from setting them off. The easy way to do this is to use a one pound hammer and it should not fire the trap. But, it will fire using a 2 lb. hammer. As you can see, determining and adjusting the poundage is important, but you must make sure the pan isn't too tight.

On long-springs you can't adjust the pan. In fact, the pan tension cannot be set at a specific poundage on any long-springs—with the exception of the very expensive specialist traps such as the Bridger #5. However, I will not address any of the specialized traps in this book because of their niche applications.

Rusting Your Traps

When you get traps new from the factory, they are shiny with a coating of grease on them. They are mass-produced and have a few things that must be done to them to get them ready for use. *The first thing you need to do is rust the traps to remove the factory grease and oil.* The reason for rusting is that, as you catch animals, the paint will wear off. As the paint wears off, the rust looks more like a natural brown instead of a shiny piece of metal guaranteed to scare off the animal.

To rust your Conibear traps, wash them in hot water and Dawn dish soap, thoroughly rinse them (remember animals can smell up to 10,000 times better than you), then stick them in your yard under some mowed grass or leaves. Water the traps once a day to keep them moist. When the traps have a light coating of rust everywhere, you are ready for the next step.

Another method for prepping your traps for rusting is to boil them for ten minutes. Pour the water off, then rust the traps.

Now, take the traps and lightly wire brush them to take off the larger rust spots. The next step is to dye the whole trap with flat black paint, speed dip or logwood dye. After painting them, hang the traps in a tree for a couple of weeks to get rid of the smell.

"The Exclusive Ones" – Red fox, Gray fox, Coyote and Bobcat

If you are planning on trapping the exclusive ones, you have to boil and rinse your traps twice.

Then, follow these steps: rust, wire brush, dye with logwood crystals and wax with trapper wax.

You can make your own dye out of different natural materials such as staghorn sumac berries (not poison sumac), black walnut hulls, and bloodroot. (See the recipe at the end of this chapter.) I prefer the logwood dye. All you do is boil the traps in the dye for 30 minutes and they come out dark black.

Waxing Your Traps

Waxing can be very dangerous. You must follow these procedures responsibly. After the traps are waxed, don't handle them with bare hands. Use gloves only from that point on.

For you people who are new to trapping, waxing traps was considered the only way to go years ago. Waxing is for leg-holds only and is good for land traps because the wax makes the trap faster, it comes up through the ground better, and it preserves the trap. If you are land trapping with leg-holds, this method is still recommended.

Please listen to me, waxing traps is used to preserve the traps and to make them lightning fast. This is something you want when you are trapping predators on land. The wax is very good to have on traps that are buried under the ground for weeks at a time. However, there is no reason to wax your Conibears or your water leg-holds.

Water leg-hold traps that are waxed pose two problems. First, the wax makes the jaws of the traps slippery and a large powerful coon can pull his foot out. Second, on bright moonlit nights, the wax is shiny and sometimes a coon will grab the jaw of the trap, and set it off without getting caught.

If you want to wax, there are two ways. The first waxing method is, while wearing clean gloves, cut the wax in small chunks, and melt it on top of the logwood dye. Make sure you scoop up any junk, such as rust particles, on top of the water first. Slowly pull the dyed traps through the wax and hang them up outside in a tree. Within an hour, you can then pack them in clean boxes. I pack mine in 18 gallon Rubber Maid "Rough Neck" plastic containers. These can be picked up at Wal-mart for $5.00 a piece. Make sure you wash them, then leave them outside to air out. After a couple of weeks, line the inside of the containers with dry brush such as grass, pine, or sage brush that will give it a woodsy smell.

The second way to wax is to dye the traps first. Once they dry, have a small, (about 2 gallon capacity) wax pot on the Coleman stove outside. Melt about 5 lbs. of wax in the pot and be very careful. The wax can catch on fire, which is why you do it outside. Have a tarp standing by to smother the fire if it happens. You want the wax just above the melting point. If it starts to smoke, lower the heat. Now dip the trap in.

At first, the trap will crack and pop until it reaches the wax temperature. In about two minutes, the trap can be slowly lifted out of the wax. I shake off the excess wax and hang the trap in a tree. This is dangerous, so be careful—no kids or dogs or anything else that could knock over the stove—can be around. The wax preserves and seals the trap from odor and makes it faster.

After reading all this you see why most beginners prefer the Conibears. I have taken brand new Conibears and just washed, rinsed, painted and gone out and caught animals with them. The only problem I had was that after a few catches, the shiny metal came through and it scared off the next animals. This is especially obvious during the early winter when ice is first forming. On the frozen water (at about ½ inch of clear ice) you can see the air bubbles of the animals (this is for beaver and muskrats) that have approached the trap. The air bubbles go right to the trap and turn to the side, instead of going through the trap. This is very frustrating because it means the animal was scared off from swimming through the trap.

Raccoons are very curious animals and they just love to grab shiny things in the water. One of the oldest methods of trapping coons is to wrap the pan of a leg-hold with tin foil. The coon will see the shiny foil and grab the pan, setting the trap off on his paw. But, if they grab the outside jaw of the trap, the trap will fire without the coon getting caught. The biggest reason you don't want to wax Conibears is that they become so touchy that sometimes while you are setting them, they will fire off and spray you with water. Or, if you are unlucky, they'll fire off and whack your hand. This safety reason is why I don't recommend waxing Conibears. I waxed Conibears one year and had traps firing off in the water as I tried to set them and I swore I would never wax Conibears again. Please, for your own safety—*Don't wax Conibears!!!!*

Homemade Trap Dye

This was sent to me from one reader who preferred this method of dyeing traps. I would like to thank Blue Skies for sending this to me.

In early fall, collect black walnut hulls that are soft and black, when they're breaking apart from the nut. Collect a gallon of them and place them in a 5 gallon pot. Fill the pot with water and bring to a boil for 30 minutes. Place your traps on a wire and lower into the pot. Remove the pot when cool and place outside. In two days, remove the traps and make sure you hang them in a tree to air dry. Once dried, pack in a clean box until you are ready to start trapping.

A warning from Blue Skies: Don't get any dye on your hands or you will wear it for a week; it won't wash out. That is why you wire the traps together and leave some wire hanging out of the pot. Then, you can just grab the wire and pull the traps out when they are done.

This is a good natural dye and scent for your traps. Wisdom from the past claims that you will catch more animals with natural dyes. Another good one is staghorn sumac berries. Do the same process as described above. I have found if you are just hobby trapping, a few traps here and there for a couple of weeks each year, this is all you need. But you still must de-grease and rust your traps as described earlier.

I have caught too many animals next to rusting farm equipment to be convinced that rust scares animals. But in a survival situation, it is good to know how to make natural dyes to keep your traps in top working order. Trapping is as subjective as anything else; some people are convinced certain ways are the best, and others believe different. I go by what works for me. Natural homemade dyes are just one more method to dye your traps that will help you get twenty years use out of the equipment. So please try it.

As mentioned at the beginning of this discussion, if you bypass any step in the preparation process, you will feel it every time you check your traps. So please, follow these instructions to the letter. And again, you are solely responsible for any and all results—good and unfortunate. I have done my best to cover the primary types of traps and sets so you can make an informed decision but I really think the majority of you will probably stick with the Conibears. If I'm wrong, please correct me.

The information I have offered you in this chapter is best summarized as follows. Select your trap and make it work for you, after all, that is why you bought it. Every trap has its strengths and weaknesses. They are just tools to help you acquire animals without hunting. And, of utmost importance is that when the game animals are hunted down, you can go to the water and trap muskrats. They really are quite tasty and the only way you can get them is by trapping. Something to keep in mind for a survival situation.

#110, #330 and a #220 Conibear (left to right)

Cage Trap; They are large, bulky and expensive. You can't carry too many but they're great for trapping coons in barns.

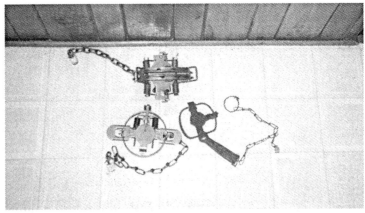

MB 650 (top), 1½ Coil-spring (left) and #1 Long-spring (right)

Water Trapping

ater trapping has different meanings to different people but can generally be defined as any trapping done at the water's edge. I have done all sorts of water trapping and will explain the different kinds.

The most important thing you should know up front is that if you are just starting out, there is no quicker way to have success than by water trapping muskrats. They are easy to trap, and if you run a couple of coon and mink traps, you will pick up extra fur along the way. Raccoons and minks, with a few sets, will not only add a little variety to the catch, but they'll also give you some more experience. Beavers are also fairly easy to trap but sometimes you run into a smart one that will drive you crazy trying to trap him.

While you should choose whatever relates to your area, for beginners, I recommend pond trapping. Ponds are great, especially on farms. The farmers don't care for the muskrats because they dig dens into the sides of ponds 6 to 8 feet back on land which causes all kind of problems from erosion to dam failure. So, the farmers are glad to have you trap the ponds. Ditches along the highways are also great spots for trapping muskrats. Rivers, streams and creeks are good spots for combination trapping; you'll find the slower moving ones are best.

I will cover muskrats, raccoons, minks, beavers and otters and discuss the various ways and means of water trapping them through the unique situations that each animal presents. And, because I like surprises and you'll never know what to expect, I will also show you some good combo sets that will take practically any different animal that comes by.

First let us define a few terms.

Deep water—Enough water to drown the intended animal you plan to trap. For instance, if you are trapping mink or muskrat, 1 to 2 feet of water is deep water. In fact, I have trapped ditches with two inches of water and caught muskrats. If you are trapping beaver and otter, deep water can be from 30 inches to 6 feet, depending on how you set up your drowning rig. For raccoons, it can be from 18 inches to 3 feet.

Drowning rig—A bent washer or a swivel with one end having a drilled hole. The swivel will go down a wire only one way. Make sure you test it before setting the trap. The one end is staked on shore and the other end is staked in deep water or you can use a sandbag and throw it in deep water. The idea is the animal will fight the trap. The only way it can go is out in deep water. One test in Canada showed the average time for a beaver in a leg-hold trap to drown is 6 to 12 minutes. I believe all animals will be drowned in that time, except muskrats, which take about 3 to 4 minutes.

Wire carrier—A device strapped on your belt that holds a full roll of wire. You can use one hand to strip out the amount of wire needed and cut it off. It is like a large fishing reel and you can crank the extra wire back into the spool for later use. This is great for people who run a lot of traps because it stops all the tangled up mess the wire roll usually gets into.

A packbasket—Wooden strips woven into a basket. This is used for carrying traps and supplies. I rarely use them because anyone who sees them knows you are trapping and trap thieves will help themselves to your catch. But if you're on private property or out of sight, it is very handy to have because the open design allows water from the wet animals to have a way to escape.

Stake—A ⅜ or ½ inch rebar with a washer welded on the top; secures the trap to hold the animal.

Yoho shovel—A special, tiny shovel, about 24 inches long, with a little blade like a garden spade except it is built tougher and welded together. This is used for digging holes and clearing paths to the trap.

Flagging material—Surveyor tape, red, orange, and blue. This is used in marshes while float trapping to identify the trap location. Again, because of trap thieves, care must be used with this. However, most thieves don't float rivers or have a boat for marshes.

Floats—Any device you make to keep the trap floating. The purpose of this is to have a trap at the correct water level so you do not have to worry about the water going up or down. More on this later.

Sifter—An 8x10 two inch high frame with steel ¼ inch mesh on the bottom for sifting dirt to prevent rocks from getting into the trap.

Lures—Ingredients added together to attract animals. Some are food based, some are gland based and some are territory based.

As mentioned in the Scouting Chapter, to understand any animal you have to study it. Go to the library and look up all the different books on the animal or animals you want to trap. There are some outstanding studies done on every animal that will provide you with valuable, detailed insight to supplement the general information I will give you.

Muskrats

This animal is probably the first animal you are going to trap. The muskrat is a valuable fur bearer and has been given a bad rap by having the word "rat" associated with it. A more appropriate name would have been marsh rabbit. The only difference between a muskrat and a rabbit is that one lives in the water. They both eat good, natural food.

While the muskrat spends most of its time in the water, it will travel a great distance on land. They have a dispersion like other animals. All this means is that in the spring and fall, the muskrats may get overcrowded. As a result, some will travel great distances over land looking for a new home on the water. That is why you will find muskrats wherever there is water.

The muskrats live in dug holes in the bank, referred to as bank dens and build round dens from 1-4 feet in diameter and around to 1-4 feet tall. These dens are built in the fall and are made out of natural materials like cattail leaves and mud.

A good rule of thumb to judge the population of the muskrats in a marsh is to count the number of dens and multiply by 5. This will give you a rough estimate. If you have 20 dens than there are about 100 muskrats there and you can safely trap about 60 muskrats a year. That is every year. This is called line management and it will ensure you have fur to trap every year.

A muskrat's main diet is cattail, sweet flag, bulrush, apples and corn. The more food, the more muskrats. They are messy eaters and leave all kinds of sign where they have been eating.

This is called a feed bed. These spots are where the muskrats go to rest and climb up on to feed. Most people who have been near water sources have seen muskrat signs and didn't know it. If there is a log half in the water or any log in the water, there will be muskrat droppings on it. The droppings are small, ½ to 1 inch long and about the diameter of rice.

The Log Set

During the early fall, before the water gets cold, cut a notch out of the logs where you see fresh droppings just below the water line. The finished notch should give you a flat area on the log about two inches below the surface. Add a dab of lure up on the log to convince the muskrat to visit it the first night. This is where you will place the trap for trapping season. Cover the fresh cut with mud and check back to make sure the muskrats are still using it.

When trapping season opens, set a #1½ L.S. in the notch, stake out to deep water. Make sure you stake the trap securely. This will take raccoons and you don't want to waste time looking for a raccoon that ran off with your trap. I take a long seasoned stick and shove it in the mud about 18 inches. Then give it 2-3 feet of wire to make sure the muskrat has plenty of room to drown. If a raccoon does somehow manage to pull the stick that is wired to the trap, he will get hung up in the brush. If you didn't have time to notch the log, then use two 2½ inch nails to keep the trap snug on the log but not so snug that the muskrat can't pull it free.

Place the trap down on the log so it is under two inches of water. With the base plate, place a nail on each side. This will hold the trap from being knocked over as the muskrat climbs on the log. But once he's caught, the trap can be pulled free so the muskrat can reach deep water.

To understand muskrats you must understand that predators are their main concern. Everything eats the muskrat—minks, raccoons, foxes, coyotes, and all the predator birds such as hawks and owls. So the muskrat tends to feed in areas where there is an overhang or in thick cattails. You will see them in the open areas but there will be more of them in the thicker areas.

In the cattails, you will sometimes find feed beds on logs or you may find floating cattails smashed down. The muskrat will climb up and peel the roots and shoots of the cattails and eat there. A good feed bed will take a lot of muskrat. If the feed bed goes through a narrow opening in the cattails you can place a Conibear there, so it is half in the water. This is so the muskrat can swim though the trap to get to the feed bed.

Wire the trap off to a stake, or place the 1½ L.S. on the platform the muskrats are landing on to climb up on the feed bed. Make sure you stake out in deep water. Place the stake so the wire and trap chain just reaches the feed bed, so the only choice the muskrat has is to go to deep water. Use cattails or sticks to narrow down the opening so the muskrat has to climb over the trap to get on the feed bed. You will be able to see the path where they are swimming up to the feed bed. If there are two paths, then set two traps.

The bank dens are where the muskrats dig into the side of the water's edge, into the bank. You will notice that the muskrat has two types of dens—abandoned and active. The abandoned dens look old and may be partially plugged with seaweed. To determine if the den is active, look for fresh mud and tracks going in the hole. Sometimes you will see pieces of dropped food. These dens are easy to trap with a #110 Conibear. Walk in the water so you don't cave it in. Once caved in, the muskrats will abandon it.

The hole will be about 4 inches in diameter and can be anywhere from 1 inch to 3 feet underwater, depending on how thick the ice freezes. Once you find a good looking hole, place the set #110 over the hole using a stick at a 45 degree angle that goes through the spring and between the set jaws. This keeps the muskrat from knocking it over. Wire off to a stake. Find the next one and repeat. You can do the same on the muskrat huts. There will be from 1 to 3 entrances into the den underwater. Use your boot to feel the holes. Then set the Conibear the same way.

The float set is another good set if you are fighting rising and falling water levels. Floats tend to work better if you make them in the summer and place them in the trapping area. This gives the muskrat time to get used to them and they will start using them on their own. The floats work because muskrats tend to dislike climbing up on exposed traps or if the water is too deep, then they swim over the trap. If this happens, you can use floats.

Just place two 4 inch diameter logs at a 45 degree angle to form a "V." Nail the one end together. Then nail a 1x4 or 1x6 at the top of the "V." Use two nails to hold the trap in place. Remember, just snug enough so that it can easily be pulled up and off. Place the float in the water and shove a long stick about 5 to 6 feet long in behind the board. Now when the water raises, the float will go up the stick and when the water goes down, the float will go down. Cover the trap with a little seaweed, just lightly enough to break up the outline. Stick a chunk of apple in the back at the "V." The muskrat will swim in to get the apple and he's caught.

Good Beginner Muskrat Sets

Some of the best sets are the easiest sets, such as using #110 Conibears in their runways. In some states, it is legal to put a trap in the muskrat's hut. In this case, I would use a #1½ L.S. My favorite muskrat set is to pull apart the hut a little and set a trap in front of it. The muskrat approaches to repair the damage and steps right in the trap. I also place #110's, baited with apple on the trigger, by a log that they are climbing onto.

You can also make a little pocket in the bank where muskrats are digging or feeding. Put a piece of apple in the back with maybe a little lure, and place a #1½ long-spring in front. Make sure you can drown them by wiring the end of the chain to a stake. Then put the stake in deeper water. The trap is heavy enough to take any muskrat down.

I heard of one guy who just trapped muskrat huts. All he did was place the 1½ L.S. where the muskrats were climbing up on the huts. He put a chunk of apple behind the trap and wired off to deep water. He ran fifty traps for one week, checking them twice a day. He was able to take 200 to 225 muskrats every year. You can't argue with success.

The man I spoke of earlier who caught 1000 muskrats in a month by trapping ditches, showed me the 6 to 8 inch culvert set. When you see a small culvert, always place a #110 in front of it. Narrow down the opening so the muskrats have to go though the trap to get into the culvert. Stabilize the trap and wire off to a stake. Make sure the trap is stabilized well because the muskrats tend to come into the pipes very quickly.

47

Trapping Muskrat under the Ice

If you have clear ice around a hut, look for a concentration of bubbles. Chop out the ice and you will feel a hole. This is their entrance to the hut and they can be found sometimes as far away as 20 feet from the hut.

Take a #110 Conibear and bait it with a carrot, parsnip or something similar that will show up underwater. Stabilize the trap under water with a stick. Have the trap wired to the stick and place it about four inches under water, near the den.

Take one spring off a #220 Conibear and you have made what is called a #210. Then chop out the runways between the main hut and feed hut. Look for pinch points between cattails. Chop out the ice. Look on the bottom of the chunk of ice for bubbles or hair roots from cattail roots. If it's real deep, set the trap on top of the muck, between it and ice. If it's shallow, feel for a groove in the bottom. Stake the trap through the spring eye with lath board 18 inches long. That way, you can adjust the height of the trap. It will stay wherever you put it on the lath board.

There are more sets, but this is plenty to get you started. Try these suggestions then experiment on your own. Stay with whatever works best for you.

Raccoons

Raccoons are plentiful and are easy to trap. However, *the key to coon trapping is holding the coon.* The best way is to drown them. Another way is with #220 Conibears but you must be very careful with them so they don't catch dogs. Everyone associates the raccoon with water and this is true but I have caught just as many raccoons on farms with no water around as I have at the water's edge.

Coons semi-hibernate in the winter. To do this, they have to put on several layers of fat. They are opportunists, which means they will go wherever there is ripe food and eat everything they can. Raccoons average in size from 10 to 40 lbs. The average trapped coon in Iowa is around 17 lbs. In my area, the Upper Peninsula of Michigan, the average weight in 1998 was around 22 lbs. on my trapline.

The coon is a vicious fighter and will kill a dog three times his size if he can reach deep water. Basically, the coon will grab a swimming dog around the head and force the dog under water. Therefore, be careful if you walk a dog around water and coons. A big male is not afraid of very much and if you corner him, he has no problem letting you know this.

#120 and #160 Conibears for Raccoons

I find the #120 useless for coons. I know some are caught in the trap every year but in my opinion, that is strictly accidental. Purposely setting for coons using the #120 will result in a lot of sprung, but empty traps. Some people like the #160 but I find that this trap is too small and the coons refuse to enter. The #220 is the best Conibear trap on the market. But, once again, if you like the #160 for coons, go for it.

#220 Conibear for Raccoons

The next set is the #220 Conibear in the bucket. You take a 5 gallon bucket with a lid and cut two slots, 7 inches long, for the springs of the #220 to slide into. Then cut a 6 inch round hole in the lid. You place the #220 Conibear in the slots all the way to the back. Place the bait in the back. Pop the lid on and place two logs on each side to keep it from rolling. Place it against a backing, like a tree or log. The bucket's back should be facing the wind and you must make sure the bucket can't roll or move back.

When the coon comes up, he is facing the opening. He will climb in to get the bait and the trap will catch him behind the ears, quickly killing him. The beauty of this set is that dogs can stick their head in without getting caught. Cats, however, will climb in so be careful where you set this trap. Also, make sure you test the trap in the bucket, with a long stick, to be certain that when it's fired it closes the whole way. Be careful, these traps will hurt if they whack you one.

If you are on private property with no dogs, you can also use a regular shovel and dig a hole 18 inches deep on the side of a steep bank. Toss a chunk of fish in the back, place the #220 Conibear in front and use two sticks to form an "X" over the trap. In freezing conditions, place a couple of small sticks under the jaws to lift the trap off the ground to keep it from freezing solid.

A friend of mine used to always set logs that cross over streams with a #220 in the middle. He caught all kinds of different animals this way, but mostly coons. He did this by pounding in 4 nails, then bending them over to hold the trap. If you do this, make sure you don't bend the nails down all the way; bend them just enough so they firmly hold the trap without disabling the jaws from closing.

Pocket Sets

The best set for coons at the water is what is called a pocket set. This set consists of a hole dug into the bank 12 to 18 inches deep at the water's edge so that water flows into the hole. The hole should be the same size as the trap. Stake on shore with a drowning wire. Stake out to deep water. Make sure you pound the stake in deep water, testing the stake to make sure it will hold. I have had some monster coons pull out stakes then climb up on land and pull out of the trap. The 1½ L.S. is placed partially in the hole with lure and a chunk of fish for bait. The trap should be wiggled down in the sand to keep it from moving. Add a little sand to the trap pan, to help blend it in.

The raccoon, mink, or muskrat will come up to the hole to get the fish and will step in the trap. This is the all time King of the water sets. I have caught everything in this set—coons, minks, muskrats, and even beavers.

The Big Hole Set

Another set I like is the big hole set. Next to a river or stream, dig a hole that will go back 12-18 inches with a couple inches of water at the mouth. Place a log, 6 to 8 inches in diameter, in the middle so you have two paths going into the hole. To create the two entrances, the log should be partially in the hole. You will need two

1½ C.S. and three stakes. Place one stake in deep water, wiring with two separate pieces of wire. Then place a stake on either side of the log set. Test your traps by ensuring the drowner slides down to deep water. Wire off to the top stake.

This way, after you catch one animal, the set is ready for the next. You will be shocked at the different kinds of doubles you will catch. For example, I have caught a muskrat and a coon, a mink and a coon and two coons. You'll find the same kind of results, or even three different animals, when you place a fish head and a coon lure all the way in the back of the hole.

To finish the set, wiggle the trap in and put just a little river sand on the pan. Just something to blend it in. One thing I do is push the river sand up to the jaws and cover the pan so the pan looks like the dry spot to step. Careful when you do it, the trap may fire, spraying you with water and sand.

Minks

Minks are not really all that difficult to trap once you understand them and there are a wide variety of materials available to help you do that. So, once again, I will provide only the basics.

The female has a home range of three to six miles and the males have a range of six to fifteen miles that could take them a week to cover. I heard about a guy who ran 300 mink traps for 30 days and caught 90 mink. He was driving over a 100 miles a day to check traps.

Granted, mink are not plentiful but you want to trap them because they are part of the weasel family and they kill everything. A male, considered large, will weigh 4 lbs. and a female will weigh less than 2 lbs. Mink kill ducks and muskrats by the truckload. I have had mink come through when I was muskrat trapping and rip apart 4-5 muskrats. That's just one mink, mind you, which shows you how destructive they can be. I have seen a mink grab a full-grown duck by the neck and kill it in seconds. Believe me, they are nature's warriors. I'm glad they don't grow to 200 lbs. We would all be in trouble.

When you are muskrat trapping you will occasionally catch a mink swimming into a muskrat den. I have caught them in a pocket set for coons and in muskrat log sets. And, even though I have caught mink in fox sets miles from water, most of your mink trapping will be done on water or near water.

I have used pocket sets as described above for coons and have probably taken the most mink with this set. The culvert set for muskrats will take mink too. If you just want to catch mink, then here are a few sets that work for me.

The Dry Overhang Bank Set

When you walk along the rivers, streams and banks you will notice where the water was real high in the spring and cut into the bank making little hollows. Mink love to explore these.

Find one of these banks underneath an overhang where it narrows down to 4-5 inches and guard the hole with a #110 Conibear. Wire off to a branch or stake in water. Spread your triggers on the #110 wide and if you are seriously after mink exclusively, connect a piece of 20-22 gauge wire from the bottom corner of the trigger to the other trigger. This will make it look like a small loop. Mink like going through this and it will increase your mink catch.

You can make the same set on any uprooted tree with a tiny opening, or a tree partially in the water where the water has washed out part of the root system and left a tiny hole for the mink to go through. Place some lure if you wish and some bait in the back of the hole. Make sure you prop the jaws off the ground with sticks under the jaws of the #110 or it will freeze solid. There is nothing more frustrating than waiting a week for the mink to come through and then finding the trap frozen to the ground when he finally does.

The Hollow Log Set

Another mink set I have always done well with is the hollow log set. Along the rivers look for a hollow log with a 4 to 8 inch opening. If you have to, move the log on a flat spot on the river so one end is in the water and the other is on land. Place a #110 Conibear in the water side of the hollow log, stabilize it and stake to deep water. The #110 should cover the hole.

On the top side, take a 1½ C.S. and dig a hole the size of the trap. Place a small wad of grass under the trap pan. This will prevent dirt from getting under the trap pan. If dirt does get under it, the trap will not fire. Wiggle the trap down so it is about ¼ inch below the surface of the ground. On the outside of the trap, pack dirt all around until the trap is solid. Then use what is called a sifter and sift a layer of dirt over the trap until the trap is completely covered and out of sight. Brush it in, so it looks natural.

Place two 3 inch diameter sticks on both sides of the trap along side the log and one small ½ inch diameter stick just in front of the trap. This way, the animal's only choice to get into the hollow log is to step over the front stick onto the trap. You can stake solid to the ground or use two stakes and a drowner if you like. Every mink and coon that comes by will have to go look into the hollow log. With a fish head and some lure inside, you will replenish your stock of fur.

Otters

Otters have beautiful fur and they are currently bringing top dollar. However, since otters are a touchy subject (they conjure up playful, free living, happy images in people) I will just give a few sets. Otters travel great distances, sometimes as a family of four or more, sometimes in pairs and sometimes alone. Their home range can be up to 40 miles and if you see fresh tracks you are usually too late. The otters are gone and won't be back for a week or two. This of course, is based on the food and lay of the land. The otter's main diet is fish and their average weight is between 15-25 lbs. They are very powerful animals. I have caught them in 1½ Coil-springs and they have drown but, I have also had them pull their foot free. #3 leg-holds or #280 to #330 Conibears are most commonly used.

Otters like to explore every side creek off a main river. My best set is to follow the small creek from the main branch until I find a spot that has been all narrowed down from a downed log. Then I place a #280 or #330 in the opening. If the water is deep, say over the trap by 1 or 2 inches, then I place a dive stick, something 2-3 inch diameter, over the trap. This will cause the otter to dive under the stick into the trap. This set will also take beaver, muskrat, and sometimes a mink.

Another set that works is the following. In fast water, take a Rapala fishing lure (the 6 inch size works best) with the hooks removed and wire it on the trigger of a #330 Conibear. Place it underwater in the current so the Rapala is moving back and forth like a minnow. Use the same "X" as before, with the sticks going through the compressed springs and the top corners of the jaws. Make sure you wire the Conibear off solid because the otter will really fight the trap. The only problem I have with the set is if a coon sees the minnow, he will dive for it. Sometimes you catch them but, most of the time, they just set off the trap.

Beavers

The beaver is a prized fur-bearer but, after the fur market crashed in 1988, people stopped trapping them. It wasn't until 1994 to the present that people started trapping them again. The beaver are super engineers and in many states their population has gone to critical mass. I think it was in 1992 that the logging companies estimated the loss of timber was $32 million. In Michigan, their numbers became so high that, in order to keep the roads open, trappers *had* to be hired. Permits to shoot beavers on sight and dynamite permits for blowing the dams were issued. But the prices for fur have come back and the trappers have stepped up and started harvesting the beaver and things are getting under control once again.

I have often been asked how many beavers can be trapped in the same spot year after year. I have found that the Canadian method—two per den—works best. If you trap two beavers, then leave, you have left plenty of seed for next year. It isn't 100% because some spots only have one or two beavers, but it is a good rule of thumb.

Dam Cross-Over Set

The beaver isn't that hard to trap unless someone has shot at him or some kid new to trapping has spooked him. The spooked beavers take a little extra from you but they, too, can be caught.

The king of beaver sets is the dam cross-over. On smaller creeks and streams, where beavers have made dams, you will find a cross over (a path they use just about every night) toward the middle. Sometimes it is hard *not* to find it because it will be all slicked up with wet mud and tracks. On the top and the bottom of the dam you can place two #330 Conibears.

Sometimes there is a nice little notch on the top of the dam where the beavers have been crossing, that is just perfect for the trap. Set the trap and cross it with the "X" through the springs and the top of the jaws. Then take 6 to 8 feet of wire and wire it off to something strong. You want the extra wire so when the beaver gets caught, he can pull the trap free and sink to deep water. This will keep the dead beaver from spooking the others.

The top trap should be half out of the water. Place a couple of 3-4 foot long sticks to form a partial "V" to guide the beaver into the trap.

On the bottom side, walk down and look for a log or branch indicating where the beavers are swimming under. That's where you place the second trap. Make the same "X" with the two sticks and wire off to something solid. If you are short on traps and have to decide where to put only one, choose the bottom side, before the pond freezes over. The bottom side is the best bet and has given me the higher percentage of catches.

Make sure you use lure. The lure's job is to convince the beaver to swim through the trap. Place the lure on a stick about 18 inches past the trap. Stick it into the dam or ground so that it is even with the middle of the trap.

The Channel Set

Walk the length of the pond and look for channels the beavers have dug into the woods or paths they have made to get out of the water into the woods. Basically, set the path with the most active beaver sign; set up the same as the set for the bottom of the dam. Look for where they have been diving under something, such as a log, branches or a stump. Then, set the trap under water so the top of the trap is even with the top of the log. If you have to, you can add a stick to make it work. Get two sticks for the "X" and wire to the log. Place lure 18 inches behind the trap and go to the next trap.

Mud Pie Set

River beavers are kind of weird. Sometimes they're easy to trap and other times they're just stubborn and go elsewhere. But the old favorite set for rivers is the mud pie set. Look for signs of active beaver. Stake out in deep water. Run your drowning wire up to shore. Take a #3, #4 or #5 trap and set it. Dig a hole, the size of the trap and just deep enough to allow the trap to sit level with the ground. Make sure there is a couple of inches of bank left next to the river. Bed the trap in by wiggling it in place and packing some dirt on the outside jaws. You don't want the trap tipsy.

Stake on shore and add your drowner. Make sure it slides to deep water. Wire off to the top stake. Place a shovel full of river mud directly behind the trap and build a mound about four inches tall. Add castor based lure and a few half-peeled Aspen branches for eye appeal and you're done.

You can set one side 4-6 inches off the center. This is because the beaver's body can be 10 inches wide so you must align the trap to the beaver's foot. The beaver swims through the hole with his front feet tucked up against his body. If you set in the water, the beaver's chest will fire the trap—all that does is scare the heck out of him. With the trap on the bank, the beaver's chest hits the bank causing him to step up with his front foot onto the trap. You will catch coon in this set too.

Log Set

The other set for river beaver that works for me is the log set. It took me a few years to figure this out and it does take some time to make, but it is worth the effort. Find a downed log, already in the river, that is 8-12 inches in diameter and 10-15 feet long. Move it off shore about a foot, parallel with the bank. You have to pound in some long sticks on each side of the log and wire them to the log to hold the log in place. Place the log up against the sticks in the water and wire off to one that is pounded in. This prevents the current or high water from moving the log.

On each end, place a #330 Conibear so the trap is half out of the water or at least two inches above the water. Use the "X" for both traps and wire off with 6 feet of wire to one of the pounded in stakes. On the bank, in the middle, add some half peeled bait sticks and lure. The beaver like to swim the edges and will think another beaver has moved in. This will prompt him to go over (right through the trap) to find out who's eating his food. If the first trap has caught a beaver, the next beaver that comes up through the space that is now open will check out the bait and swim out the other end into the last trap.

The leg-hold really comes in handy when trapping smart beaver. You need a #3 or larger trap, a drowner, two stakes and wire. Stake out in deep water. Remember, a beaver swims with his front feet tucked up against his body. When his chest hits the bank, he sticks out his foot to walk. So to catch him you need some poke sticks. Find a spot where the beavers are coming out of the water and dig a trap bed on the bank.

Stake one stake in deep water and run wire up to the top stake. Place the drowner on the wire. Make sure it only goes down, not up! Set the trap and wiggle it in the mud so that it is solid, not tipsy. Place small poke sticks so they stick out from the trap about 2 to 3 inches. Place the lure 18 inches behind the trap. Beavers have a wide body. The beaver will smell the lure and swim over to see what is going on. They will hit the poke sticks and place their foot out into the trap to climb up. The trap will fire and the beaver will be caught by its front leg. The beaver will dive for deep water and the drowner will hold him on the bottom. In 6 to 12 minutes the beaver will drown.

This set works really well where the beavers are trap shy of the #330 Conibear.

Water trapping can be very basic or quite complex. My recommendation: start with, or freshen up on, the basics and begin experimenting with some of the more sophisticated methods as you gain more confidence and experience. You will learn new techniques along the way; techniques that I may have touched on or may not yet know myself. In that case, please send them my way—they may find their way to my next edition.

50-pound beaver in a #330 Conibear.

Otter in a #330
Conibear.

Mink caught in a #110 Conibear. Notice the small opening, it's perfect
for a #110.

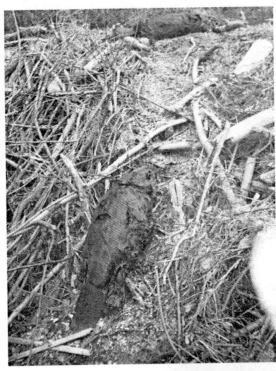

Double catch on a beaver Dam Cross-over set.

#330 Conibear Channel Set with dive log; two beavers were caught in this set.

Coon caught in a leg-hold in an Upper Pennisula, Michigan culvert set.

Land Trapping

ore has been written on land trapping than I could ever hope to accomplish in this chapter, so once again, my intention is to cover the hands-on basics. Land trapping can be very frustrating and most people who start trapping on land first, get very discouraged. When land trapping, to catch an animal you have to narrow its world down to four inches. In addition, rain washes away your dirt, traps freeze to the ground, animals come up and step everywhere but on the pan of the trap, and invariably, some smart fox or coyote will come along and dig up your trap.

This last point, that a fox or coyote will dig up your trap, is the main problem faced by most new trappers. When I first started, I didn't understand the big deal. I thought that if the fox digs by my trap, then I should catch him. I learned differently. The leg-holds work when the animal steps on the pan of the trap. When an animal digs, he is lightly brushing off the dirt that is covering the trap. Some just dig until part of the trap is exposed; others dig and then flip the trap. It all depends on the animal.

You can prevent this by properly bedding your trap and by following the one fundamental rule of trapping: *You and your equipment must be clean and scent free.* (I store my equipment in Rubber Maid "Rough Necks.") When trapping, don't wear the same boots that you wore when you gassed up your vehicle and make sure your vehicle is free of any coffee and pop spills, oils or any foreign odor that will scare the animals. Wear clean cotton, leather or rubber gloves. When you are walking out on the trap line, walk through mud puddles or any type of water to wash the scent off your boots. One other thing: don't smoke or chew tobacco while running traps.

Following are some of the key terms related to Land Trapping that you need to know.

Lures—Ingredients added together to attract animals. Some are food based, some are gland based, and some are territory based.

Urine—Collected from different animals; sprayed on the trap bed in the Dirt Hole set and on a rock or stick for the Urine Post set to attract and remove suspicion from the approaching animal. Some urine works for all animals but most people use the urine of the specific animal they are trapping; fox urine for fox trapping and so on.

Gland lures—Collected from the animal and aged. This is very effective on flat sets.

Steel stakes—18-36 inches long, ⅜ or ½ inch rebar with a washer welded to the top. Never weld on the bottom side. A hammer is used to pound the stake in. I started with a 2-lb. machine hammer but progressed to a high rolling hammer. Some people like the 24-oz. carpenter hammer and use the claw to help dig the trap bed, others use a 3-lb. masonry hammer and weld a piece of flat stock on it.

Double stake swivel—For coyote trapping or fox trapping in coyote country, it is designed to pound in two stakes at a 45-degree angle so they cross. This prevents coyotes from pulling the stake out.

This also prevents some thieves from stealing your trap.

Swivels—Added in the chain to prevent the animals from rolling and kinking the chain up.

Sifter—An 8x10 two inch high frame with steel ¼ inch mesh on the bottom for sifting dirt to prevent rocks from getting into the trap.

Bedding the trap—After you dig the trap bed, you place the trap in the bed and pack dirt around the outside edges so the trap doesn't wobble or move in case the animal steps on the jaw of the trap instead of the pan. This is very important! Pack that trap in tight and then push on the outer edge, if the trap moves or lifts up, then pack it some more until the trap is rock solid.

Pan covers—Several different things such as crumbled up wax paper, paper, steel screens, *(Caution: Never use Galvanized screens)*, etc, used to prevent dirt from getting under the pan of the trap. In a pinch, you can use balled up grass stuffed under the pan. Just don't pack it so tight that the pan won't go down. I use steel screens. If you choose to use them also, you have to adjust your pan tension to 2 pounds.

Fox trapping

Red Fox

The red fox is a smart little animal. With an average weight of 6-12 lbs., they appear bigger because of their full fur coat. The fur has different color phases ranging from natural orange to mixed gray brown color. Some fur even has some black.

Their natural predators are coyotes and when still small, they are also preyed upon by eagles and larger hawks. They are naturally nervous and cautious. One study found that the fox's normal travel is 30 feet from the wood line or hedge row. Their main diet is mice, insects, berries, house cats, and the carcasses of large prey animals that died from other causes such as getting hit by a car.

The fox is similar to a dog in that it will scent an area with urine.

Have you ever walked a dog and had it stop to smell a tree? The fox has the same instinct. He will mark a spot so that others that come by will smell what has been there.

The Dirt Hole Set

The king of the fox sets is the dirt hole set. There are 100 different ways you can make this set but, I will give you two ways and you can modify it to your taste. If you're trapping farms, find an area where a fence line comes together with another, or where a dirt road is coming from the woods into the field. Remember, you must pay attention to the wind. The back of your set must be aligned with the wind so the lure scent goes across the field. About 30 feet out, look for some kind of backing—a rock, a chunk of wood, a small slope, something that will back up the hole. Sometimes you can find a small bank at the edge of the field next to the woods.

Approach the area and carry everything you need to make the set. (A 5 gallon bucket works well.) You don't want to scent up the area by walking back and forth several times. Have your sifter, hammer, trap, pan cover, and stakes in the bucket. On the outside of the bucket, strap a fanny pack on to carry your lures. Don't carry your lure or bait in the bucket. This will cause digging.

Now, with your trowel or garden shovel, dig a 3-4 inch diameter hole at a 45-degree angle 12 inches deep. As you pull the dirt out, place it in the sifter. Once the hole is dug, dig your trap bed.

At first, the easiest way is to set the trap, put the pan cover in place, stick the trap down and look at the size area you need to dig.

The #1½ C.S. is a perfect trap for the Dirt Hole Set. Dig out an area the size of the trap, maybe two inches deep. Break up the ground and loosen the dirt. Place the stake off to one side and pound it in so it is underground. Place the set trap in the bed and pack it in tight. The trap should be ¼ to ½ inch below the ground. The pan should be dead center with the hole, 3 inches back from the lip of the hole. Once the trap bed is solid, take your sifter and cover the trap up with dirt until the ground is level or there is a slight depression by the trap pan. The dirt will cover the pan first and make a mound. Place your trowel on the side and carefully level the trap in. Take clumps of grass and pack them along the two sides of the trap, up to the hole forming a "V." Tear the area up behind the trap and make it look like a fox just dug it up. The only smooth spot should be over the trap.

The finished set should be 18 inches of dirt behind the trap, in a widening "V." Place your bait in the hole, cover it with a tuft of grass and add your lure to the grass. You can use bait only, but bait and lure will bring them in. If you have urine, spray the area you were standing or kneeling on. Clean up and make sure no human tracks can be seen. Step back and look over the set. If everything is level and the hole is open, then leave.

After that, check the trap from a distance. Just make sure the trap hasn't been fired off by a deer. If you can, use binoculars. After you make a catch, approach the animal and shoot him in the head with a .22 short. Immediately after you shoot, remove the animal and carry him away about 30 feet so he can bleed away from the set. Place his head down so the blood won't get in the fur.

Remake the set. First, use your trowel and clean up all the blood and throw it away. Make sure the trap is clean of blood, scrape it with weeds and then toss the weeds away. Dig out the hole and dig up the trap bed. Reset the trap, bed the trap, sift the dirt over. This is very important as the area will be all torn up. Place the backing in place and use all the debris to make the "V" again. Once you catch a fox, all the fox in the area will come by to see what he was doing there.

The Flat Set

The flat set is hard for beginners to understand but it is a very good set for the finicky fox.

No bait is used—rather it is based on the theory that just like a dog, a fox will mark his territory. Use gland lure or urine as the attraction. This set is best against a good backing like a bank or a large rock and the trap should be right next to this backing.

Dig the area up. Be careful to remove the top soil for the final sifting of the trap. Dig the trap bed, set, stake, prepare your pan cover and bed the trap. Now cover the trap up with dirt when you are at ground level. Sift the topsoil back on the trap. Place tiny ¼ inch diameter sticks on either side of the trap. Spray about 1 oz. of urine, or a lima bean size of gland lure on the rock or bank. Make sure there is no human sign remaining and walk away.

Urine Post Set

When they come in from the field or at a fence corner, foxes will mark their territory. The purpose of this set is to make it look like the fox just marked the area. You will do this on a small rock or stick about six to twelve inches tall. This set is made just like the flat set, except instead of using a bank or large rock, you are using a bush or stick. Make the set just as described above except leave the ground bare and torn up. Again, the idea is to make it look like the fox marked the area, then scratch it up a little. Spray 1-2 ozs. of urine on it. Make sure the smell goes over the trap. Remove all human signs.

These three sets—dirt hole, flat and urine post—have trapped thousands of foxes all over the U.S. You can modify the dirt hole by changing the angle, making a larger diameter, spreading out more dirt to make a larger area, etc. Try different ways. Find out what works for you, and stick with it.

Gray fox

I think the gray fox has the best colors—gray, silver, red, brown and white. In hard times, they would make a nice fur-lined jacket. With an average weight of about 4 to 8 lbs, the gray fox is a smaller fox. They have a smaller foot and a more slender leg and are more of a brush fox or southwestern fox.

Hound hunters report that, when chased, the grays will climb trees to avoid the dogs. Their diet is about the same as red foxes. Anywhere there are farms and pine trees there should be gray foxes. Out west you will find them in the dry washes. The males are quite respectable in a trap; they will charge and try to attack you when you get close.

The same three sets—dirt hole, flat and urine post—work for catching grays as well as reds; the only significant difference is location. The red fox stays more in the open farm fields and while the grays hunt farms, they prefer woods close by. They travel in pairs or alone.

Picking gray fox locations depends on where you are in the U.S. and is directly related to what it likes to eat. East of the Mississippi, the grays will be in pines and brushy areas, wood lots in between farms, old logging roads and clear cuts that are just starting to grow. In the Western states, more particularly in the southwest, they prefer dry washes and sage brush with rabbits and quails. The gray has a small foot so try to use a 1½ C.S. unless you have a lot of coyotes. In that case, use a 1¾ with offset jaws.

Coyotes

There is an old Indian legend that says the coyote will be the last animal on the earth. For sure, there is no other animal that is as adaptable as the coyote. Wherever this animal is, all over the lower 48 and up through Canada and Alaska, he flourishes. Western coyotes are from 20-35 lbs. but the northern states, east of the Mississippi have had some real Giants. There are reports from Michigan, New York, Maine and Vermont that the coyotes have reached up to 65 lbs.

The coyotes are generally gray in color with black highlights on the back. But, there have been coyotes caught with different color phases; some pure black, some light yellow and some darker gray. The western coyote has the best color fur. It is almost silver in color. The animal is tough, smart, strong and one of the hardest animals to hold in a trap. If there is a weak spot in your trap, chain, stake, or swivel, the coyote will find it and break it.

I have had coyotes blow the jaws right out of a #1½ C.S. And once again, to understand coyotes, you must understand their food, which is primarily deer. In fact, one study done in Pennsylvania found that 67% of the coyote diet is deer. Here in Michigan, packs of up to thirteen have been watched attacking deer in the winter. A pack that size can really thin out a deer herd in a hurry when the snow is deep. Out west, they travel in pairs or family units of around six. The coyotes are very effective hunters and only during the winter do they approach large bait in great numbers.

During the Fall, they can still be caught in dirt holes using bait. You must understand coyotes. Their hunting range is typically on a 9-day cycle. This of course is based on food supply. To give you an idea about coyotes, look at the following example. To catch a hundred foxes, you would have to run a hundred traps over most of a county for 30 days. To catch a hundred coyotes, you would have to run 300 traps over three counties for 30 days. This is just a rough estimate to illustrate the difference. The coyote is the most adaptable creature around.

In the early '90s, Arizona outlawed trapping. When it happened, I wrote to an Arizona newspaper and stated that within five years the coyote would lose their fear of man and start attacking children. I was wrong. It only took two years before the first attack. Coyotes will kill and do kill dogs regularly. Dogs and house cats in states that outlawed trapping will keep having more and more problems being grabbed right in front of the owners and fences will continue to be jumped in order to kill dogs in yards. Small children will be attacked more and more also. This is simply based on facts. Remember the rule: Predator or prey.

When trapping coyote, use the same sets for fox except, *make your dirt holes larger and use larger traps.* The trap sizes for coyotes are #1¾ , #2 and #3 C.S. or L.S. Most professional coyote trappers use the #3 with laminated jaws, off sets, and 4 coils. I have caught coyotes in #1¾ C.S. but, I have welded a bubble on the jaws of the trap where they go through the frame. This prevents the jaws from being pulled out. If I were serious and only wanted coyotes, I would use nothing but the modified #3 C.S.

The critical aspect when you are coyote trapping is the trap placement. When you are fox trapping, you make the set with the trap close to the hole. With coyotes, you want the trap back 8 inches from the hole. That is, the pan center should be 8 inches back from the hole. This places the trap in line with the coyote when he comes up to the set. Make 4-8 inch diameter dirt holes with 24 to 36 inches of "V" out from the hole. Make sure you have a good backing and a couple of rocks to help guide the coyote's foot onto the trap pan.

On the flat set, do the same as for foxes except, instead of having the trap snug up against the rock, move the trap out 8 inches, pan center from the backing. Use rocks or sticks on the outside of the trap jaws to help guide the foot over the trap. Move the trap out 8 inches from the stick. Coyotes will go up to smell what the foxes are doing.

Remember, coyotes will be around for centuries to come. Don't worry about them—they will survive and adapt to whatever the future holds.

Bobcats

Bobcats are similar to coyotes but they do not have the numbers. Bobcats range in average weight from 20 to 35 lbs. The largest I ever heard of was a 69 pounder in Utah. Here in Michigan the unofficial record is 58 lbs. The western cats have the better fur with more spots and nicer colors. The bobcat's main food is rabbits. The earliest study conducted on bobcats and lynxes was done by the Hudson Bay Fur Company in the 1700s, in Canada. The finding: there was a direct relationship between the snowshoe hare's population and the wild cat population. It is quite simple. Their main food is rabbit. So, when the rabbit population is up, so is the wild cat population. Here in Michigan, most of the bobcats are trapped in the cedar swamps, again, where the rabbits reside.

Out west, the bobcats prefer the rock ledges and dried out stream beds. Find the food and you find the cats. Bobcats don't have the same acute sense of smell that the foxes or coyotes have but they can be lured in the right spot. The bobcat can have a range from six to nine days to cover his territory. They mostly travel alone. I have waited for bobcats to come back through for up to two weeks. Then, after I pulled the traps, I have had them come back up four weeks later. This I think is because of an isolated food source they found, like a deer wounded by a bow hunter.

The Cubby Set

The king of the bobcat sets is the cubby set, which is basically a box. This can be made with a #220-#330 Conibear or a #2 or #3 C.S. or L.S. This set is made out of sticks pounded in the ground to form a box 23 to 30 inches long. Back it against a tree. Cover the top with pine boughs. Stick logs around the sides if you have to reinforce it. Place a beaver tail and head in the back.

Place the #220 or #330 in the front door, about 2 inches back in. Make sure you place two sticks under the jaws to prevent the jaws from freezing to the ground.

Use two sticks to form the "X" over the trap, through the compressed springs and the top of the jaws of the trap. This will stabilize the trap. Take some pine boughs and break up the outline of the trap; leave a few hanging down on the top third of the trap. Wire to something solid.

If you are using leg-holds, then dig the trap bed just inside the opening and bed the trap. If you are in freezing weather, then place wax paper above and below the trap. Bed the trap using cattail flowers to cover the trap and a light coat of pine needles to blend it in. Make sure you have the trap and the opening narrowed down so the only way to get in is over the trap. Place a stepping stick on each side of the trap to form a rough square. The sides of the cubby walls and the two sticks will form this.

Place a castor based beaver lure in the back and the bobcat will think something else killed the beaver and stashed it there for a later meal. I make this set in cedar swamps next to beaver dams. Out west, you can make the set out of rocks. Sometimes, I add a bird wing wired to the top of the cubby so it hangs down in the back. When you look in, at bobcat level, it hangs down about halfway. Any wind will move this, which may be why the cat decides to go in.

Dirt holes and flat sets will work. Just make sure you set them as you would for coyotes. Pay attention to location and the bait they like. Venison, beaver, and fish have worked the best for me.

The main concern with bobcat trapping is keeping your trap working by brushing the snow out.

Raccoons, Opossums, and Skunks

Any fox trapper will tell you the best coon, possum, and skunk set is a dirt hole made for fox. It is true that the dirt hole will take all three of the above animals. But, if you want to concentrate on each one, here are a few sets to help you out.

If you are farm trapping, coons will have a trail leading into the field. Sometimes, this trail is so obvious I can't understand how anyone would miss it. Coons will drag corn stalks and cobs along the trail. Just walk the edge of a cornfield and look for the trail. Once you find the trail, set it with a #220.

Just find a spot where the trail narrows down. Set the #220 in the trail and place a branch over the top to keep the coon from jumping over the trap. Just like water trapping, use two sticks through the compressed spring to form the "X" and a couple of sticks under the jaws to prevent freezing and you're in business. You can set two to four traps on the same trail. Make sure you wire the trap off. And don't ever make this set where a dog is near by. When on private property, make sure you get the farmer's permission to use Conibears on the ground. This trap will kill dogs and house cats.

If dogs are a problem just set a #1½ C.S. in the trail. Make the trail set just like a flat set, saving the topsoil for the finish, and sift. Don't stake near anything the coon can grab to help him power out. Use two sticks so that, as the coon approaches from either way, he steps over the stick on to the trap pan. Don't use leaves for covering. Leaves are slippery, especially when wet and the coon can pull his foot free.

71

Raccoons
The 5 Gallon Bucket Set (for raccoons)

This is basically a #220 in a dog proof bucket. Take a 5 gallon bucket and cut a slot on each side 7 inches long, just wide enough for the compressed spring to slide to the back. Cut a 6 inch round hole in the lid. Test the trap with the lid on to make sure that when it's fired, it closes all the way. Use a long stick to test it, these traps hurt if you get your hand in one. Place the bucket along the trail with the wind coming from the back of the bucket. (For average to large dogs.)

Use fish or corncobs for bait, add lure and place the trap in the bucket. Pop the lid on. Use a tree for a backing and two 4-6 inch diameter logs on both sides to prevent it from rolling. Wire to the tree. It works best if you pre-place the buckets before trapping season and train the coons to walk into the bucket and get a free meal. Then when the season opens, you will catch coon the first night.

Opossums (Possums)

Possums' fur is gray in color. They stink sometimes because they love to prowl the countryside and pounce on and viciously attack anything that is already dead. Possums range in size from 6-10 lbs. They have a set of teeth equal to a coon and, when cornered, a big male can put up quite a fight. They are everywhere and should be trapped down every Fall because they are major "egg eaters," which means they eat the eggs of game birds and song birds. The possum, coon and skunk all chase the mother bird off the nest and eat the eggs. I heard of one farm where the pheasant population took a tremendous dive in just two years. The owner hired a trapper thinking that the foxes were eating all the pheasants. In two weeks on 40 acres, the trapper trapped 54 possums. The next year the pheasants started to come back. So, if your favorite farm has fewer pheasants to hunt, maybe you should start trapping.

One more reason for trapping is that it helps keep everything in balance. When I was a teenager and possums were bringing about $3.00 on the average (similar to $10.00 today). I would wait until the first snow on a warm night then, I would load up the five or six #220s

I had and track possums to their dens. It is quite simple. All I did was track the possum to the den and set the trap over the hole. I used just one stabilizing stick and two freeze sticks wired to something solid, like a tree. By the end of the day, I would have all six traps set. I could take from 2 to 6 possums from each den. When I was 15, that was good money.

The bucket set for coons will work on possums and so will the trail set. Dirt holes work well also. Just make the set with the same care that you would for fox because you might catch a fox or a coon first.

Skunks

Why in the world would anyone want to trap skunks on purpose? Well, as previously stated, they are egg eaters, they can easily become over populated and have been known to spread rabies.

They are edible, and the tip of the day, their fat rendered down makes a fine gun oil. Skunk fur makes a nice warm hat and most people leave you alone if you're wearing one because, if they think you are crazy enough to trap, skin, tan, and sew a skunk into a hat, then you are too crazy for them. Some people have no sense of humor.

In addition, if someone is bothering you, a couple of skunk glands on their exhaust manifold will teach them to leave you alone. This is for information purposes only of course. I would never do something like that.

Their fur is nice and silky and many a trapper saved the farm during the depression by trapping skunks. There was a big fashion demand for "civet cats" (skunks) in Europe during the depression. Skunks were bringing $2.00 on the average. That was big money back then when the average wage in the factory was $15.00 a week.

Skunks live in dens under old buildings, rock piles and brush piles. I have trapped some farms and took as many as 8 skunks in fox traps. Shoot the skunk in the lungs with a .22 short hollow point. If the critter sprays, leave him in the trap until the next day. If you reset the trap, the skunk smell will guarantee that your loving wife will not allow you in the house for the night. Women just can't appreciate a good Mountain man nowadays.

The #220 over their dens works well as does the dirt hole. Have fun in your skunk trapping.

Weasels

There are two types of weasels in North America—the long tail and the short tail weasel. The short tail weasel has been called ermine. In the winter months, both species turn a beautiful white to match the snow. Generally, they turn to the white phase when the snow is permanently on the ground. In the Upper Peninsula of Michigan, the change happens about November 15 every year. You do not want to trap the weasel when they are in the half-change state because the fur is worthless.

Weasels' main diets are mice but the little blood-sucker can take down rabbits. Chicken farmers who are raided by a weasel will find the dead chickens with small teeth marks on the neck. When the chickens in the coop panic, a blood bath frenzy breaks out as the weasels' attack will continue just for the fun of the chase. I have talked with farmers who have lost up to eight chickens in one night from one weasel.

Trapping the little weasel is not hard because the animal is fearless and the trap does not bother him. A #1 long-spring or #1½ long-spring is the trap of choice. You want to slightly bend the dog down so it fires on only 2 ounces of pressure.

I normally set up under brush piles and use a piece of beaver meat or muskrat meat for bait. I pin the meat to the ground and make a small cubby so the only way to the meat is over the trap. To blend the trap in, use one small leaf placed inside the jaws covering the pan. Look for a spot with an overhang of brush to keep snow off the trap. Make sure you wire the trap off thoroughly because raccoons and mink hunt these brush piles, also.

Hollow Log Set

This is another favorite weasel set. Block off one end of the log if it's on the ground, place bait in the back and place the trap inside the log. Take and chop a trap bed if you have to and use the fine sawdust to light coat the trap. Wire the trap outside to a stout branch.

The Box Set

This is the old time favorite. Make a plywood box about 6 x 8 with a top you can slide to one side. Cut a 1½ inch hole dead center on one of the 6-inch sides. Place the trap right in front of the hole. The trap chain is nailed to the box. The bait is placed in the back of the box. When the animal jumps in the box, he lands on the trap pan. This set is a very good method for keeping traps working in freezing and snowy conditions.

I have used the #110 Conibear with bait right on the trigger before. It works well for the long tail weasel but I had too many misses on the short tail so I stopped using it. I now only use the leg-holds. Once caught in a leg-hold, weasels quickly die.

One animal I have never trapped is a pine marten. However, I read that you can trap one the same way as a fisher using #120 Conibears and a plywood box on a leaning pole. The box is 5 x 5 x 18 inches. Two notches are cut in the side of the box to support the trap. Bait is placed in the back.

Fishers

The fisher is one of the larger members of the weasel family. They are one of the few predators that are capable of wiping out the prey animals in a given area. Nature has provided them with claws for climbing and digging. A squirrel is no match in a tree against a fisher. Fishers, like their cousin the weasel, have no real fear of traps.

Nevertheless, I always make my sets with the same care as I would for fox and coyote. Once again, you never know what will come by your set first. The two favorite sets of mine for the fisher are the cubby set and the leaning pole set.

The Leaning Pole Set

The leaning pole set is made with a large downed tree. I prefer the 6 to 8 inch sizes. Wedge the tree in between two standing trees so that four feet is sticking out in the air. Use two nails to hold the #220 Conibear in place. Set the trap and place it on the log. Make sure you are past the trees about 10-12 inches. This is because sometimes the fisher will climb one tree to get the bait and miss the trap.

Use one nail and mark a spot on each side of the inside jaw spread. Remove the trap and pound in the nails. Bend the nails slightly out. Now open the #220 slightly and squeeze onto the nails. When you are finished, the #220 Conibear should be held firmly in place but the jaws must be free to fire shut.

Place the bait past the trap. I like a piece of beaver meat nailed to the tree. Cover the bait to keep ravens and crows out of your traps. Wire the trap to the tree and remember to take the safety off.

This set will take raccoons, fishers, and bobcats.

The Cubby Set (for Fishers)

I make this cubby set with logs and rocks and close off an area about two feet long. Use a tree for a backing, about 2 feet high. Use pine boughs on top to cover the whole cubby. Narrow down the front so that you have a small opening about 8 inches wide that widens out to about 18 inches once inside. Place a #3 Bridger in the narrow down spot. Make sure it is under the pine bough to keep the snow off the trap. Place the bait and lure in the back.

This set will take foxes, coyotes, raccoons, bobcats, and fishers.

Leg-Holds (aka "Foot Restraining Devices") and Trail Sets for Coons and Beaver

Leg-holds can also be used on trail sets. Look for a trail entering the field from the woods and follow it for a short distance. You are looking for a narrowed down spot—a small tree, a branch they are stepping over, a bush they duck under—something that narrows the path down. Dig a trap bed and set and stake the trap. Sift dirt over and make the area look like before. Place a stepping stick on both sides of the trap. A 1 inch diameter stick will work. The animal will step over the stick into the trap. This is a good set for smart coons.

Remember, to prevent freezing on your leg-holds, use wax paper on the bottom and top of the trap, use cattail tops for freeze proofing and a very light coating of dirt over the top. In addition to wax and dirt, anti-freeze spread on the dirt also works for freeze proofing. The anti-freeze I am referring to is Polypropylene glycol, not ethyl glycol.

By now, I am sure you have gained a better appreciation for the value and purpose of land trapping. Just have fun and don't be alarmed— every trapper has to deal with critters that mess with their traps. If you encounter a really smart one, leave him for seed to restock the fur for next year.

Fisher caught in a modified 1¾ Northwoods in the Upper Pennisula of Michigan. It was released unharmed; Fisher season was closed.

Steel stake and a grapple or drag.

1–24" by ¹/₂" rebar stake
2–Double stake swivel
3–Modified chain swivel
4–#2 BMI pro K-9

Leaning pole set using a #220 Conibear for racoon, fisher and bobcats.

78

Cubby set for a bobcat. Notice the trap is between two horizontal stepping sticks.

The Flat set–start; Note the large rock is used as backing.

The Flat set–finished; gland lure has been placed on two spots on the rock so it will flow better in the air currents.

Making the Dirt Hole Set

1. Pick the spot. Note the bank is used for backing.

4. Bed the trap.

2. Dig the hole and place dirt in the sifter.

5. Sift dirt over the trap and place guide sticks.

3. Set the trap.

6. Lure the hole.

80

5. Snaring

Snaring has been around for centuries. The older styles used light wire and required a straining device to put pressure on the snare to keep it tight. You may recognize the older style of snaring (the traditional spring pole snare) from the movie scene where the rabbit runs into a snare and then the tree that was bent over springs up and pulls the animal off the ground.

The spring action was necessary to make sure the rabbit couldn't wiggle out of the snare.

But, one thing I have noticed is that most survival manuals show all these spring pole snares with plain wire, which is useless on medium to large animals because of its low breaking point. These look really good in the illustrations but I have often wondered why there are only drawings, never actual photos, of them. Furthermore, none of these drawings have ever shown an animal being caught in one. Curious, isn't it? Well, let me tell you about the spring pole snare. The nice small sapling you need to use as a spring pole is never near the trail you want to set. It looks good in the movies but in reality, a modern snare with a locking device is far superior to any spring pole snare. Using plain wire limits you right off the bat. A medium size animal like a coon can and will break the wire. Why would anyone go through all that work when a modern snare is available?

Snaring takes a little practice before you get the hang of it, but the knowledge and experience is useful to have on hand. Once you know how to snare, you'll see that it is basically following five steps:

1. Pound the stake
2. Set the support wire
3. Wrap the snare around the support wire
4. Open the snare to the correct size
5. Center in the trail and move to the next one.

You can snare anything—from rabbits to deer. There is even a foot snare bear trap sold in Maine. But if you ever use one of those traps, be very careful when you're checking it. Of course, this holds true for checking any traps. I have reached for muskrats (that I was sure had drowned) caught in foothold traps. Imagine my surprise when those "dead" animals came alive and attacked my hands.

If a snare catches a dog, it usually doesn't kill him because dogs are used to being restrained and they will sit down and wait for you. This is just in general, of course, because it is possible that a particular dog won't stop fighting. In that case, he will end up choking himself.

The old trappers used light, 16 or 18 gauge, wire for small animals but soon learned that it was not very effective on larger animals. Once caught, the larger animal simply fought the wire until he broke free. The trapper started weaving the wire together like rope to increase the strength. This works, but animals tend to shy away from a large loop.

Snares of today are inexpensive (ranging in price from $12.95-$23.95 per dozen) and have been greatly improved. They have a self-locking device that is designed to only go one way and tighten on the animal's neck. The harder the animal fights the snare, the tighter it becomes. This eliminates the need for a spring pole and frees the trapper up to place snares where the animals are without having to worry about a finding a spring pole. Because of this, the trapper can set more snares in a day. In fact, once you get used to snaring you can easily set 100 or more a day.

Snares are now made out of aircraft cable, of varying thickness, up to fifty times stronger than ordinary wire. This feature makes them very reliable but if the animal really fights the snare, the cable can become so kinked up it is of no further use. The snare also has a loop on the end that is swiveled to allow the animal to roll without breaking the wire. This loop is called the stake end and is used with a ½ inch piece of rebar, 24 inches long.

The next improvement is a support collar. This is used with #9 wire to support the snare at the proper height. The locking device allows the snare to close quickly and holds the animal tight. The modern snare is fast and strong enough to hold a deer which is why some states have laws that require a deer stop—a piece of metal crimped on the snare to prevent it from fully closing tighter than 2½ inches. This allows a deer caught by the leg to pull out without being harmed. Also, they make some snares with a breakaway device so that if it catches a deer by the neck, the deer can break free. Once the deer breaks away, the snare falls apart.

There are three disadvantages to snares. The first is that they blend in so well you can walk right by them. So you better make darn sure you know where you set them. You can work a flagging system with surveyor tape—just be careful because the fur thieves will learn what you are doing and help themselves to your catch. The best thing to do is to make up your own marking system with something like a stick against a tree that points to the snare. Use whatever you like but if you don't have a terrific memory, mark them somehow. I have spent far too much time looking for snares because my great memory failed me.

Second, you must realize that snares are only good for a few catches before the animals have kinked up the wire so bad you can't re-use them. That is why I recommend the Conibears. Twenty years from now they will still be catching fur.

The other problem with snaring can be people. Here in Michigan, we are very restricted with snares; only underwater snares can be used. This law seems to be related to the false notion that trappers are poachers and if land snaring were allowed, we would go crazy snaring deer. Snares have been outlawed here for 50 years or more and even with the advent of deer stops, this law doesn't seem to have a chance to be overturned. The Michigan DNR has formulated its trapping regulations without giving enough consideration to the fact that trapping is the most important method for controlling predators.

With trapping, the predator numbers stay at the carrying capacity of the land and more game animals flourish, including deer. In deep winter snow, coyotes are much easier to snare than to trap. According to one study done in PA, 67% of the coyote's diet is deer. It only stands to reason, then, that if coyotes are trapped in the winter, there will be more deer to hunt. Less coyotes equals more deer. Another study done out west found that a single coyote kills and eats 100 rabbits a year. You do the math. Are you getting a sense of the importance of trapping?

Snares come in different sizes and lengths and I have discussed a few of the basic ones that will work well for you as you start out. To prepare snares, boil them in water with one cup of baking soda per gallon and place them outside to weather. The snares don't really rust, but they will become dull after seven or eight days. Like all traps, you don't want your snares to be shiny.

Small Game Snare

This snare comes in 4 feet lengths and is made out of $\frac{1}{16}$ aircraft cable. This is for small game like rabbits, squirrels, and ground hogs. You can set them in trails, dens, and for squirrels on branches going between two trees. They retail for about $12.95 per dozen and $119.95 for 10 dozen.

84

Medium Game Snare

The next snare is versatile and can be used for several different animals including fox, coon, coyote, and beaver. It has the following features: Sure-lock, support collar, #9 swivel that takes a standard ½-inch, 24 inch long rebar stake, ³⁄₃₂" cable and, if needed, deer stops can be added at no extra charge. They come in a standard 5 foot length. Their price is $15.95 per dozen and $130 for 10 dozen. This is a good all around snare to use and have on hand.

Pigtail Supports

Pigtail supports are made to support your snare at the desired height off the ground. Another option available is to use # 9 gauge wire to support the snare. I have used 11-gauge wire for the support, but it takes a little monkeying around to get it at the correct height. When using wire for the support, bend about two inches on the bottom and make a special wire driver out of rebar. A wire driver is a 1/2 rebar with a groove cut in the bottom to hold the #9 wire. Once pounded in the ground the wire will support the snare without moving. Remove the driver for the next snare. Make sure you use a good ½-inch rebar stake to hold the animal. You will love its efficiency.

The height off the ground, at which you set the snare, varies with the animal. A coon loop is 8-inches wide, 3 inches off the ground with an overall height of 11 inches. This is rough of course because different parts of the country have different size coons. If you come up and the loop is closed with no animal, your loop is too big.

Coyote snares are made with a 12-inch loop—8 inches from the ground and 20 inches off the ground at the top. You will have to experiment a little. I'm giving you ballpark figures. If you are after fox only, then you would lower the snare so it is 4 inches off the ground and 12 inches at the top with a 8-inch loop. If you are in real windy areas, you can keep the snare positioned correctly on the path by tying off the snare with a brown thread and a stick opposite the support side. The snared animal will quickly break the thread and the snare will tighten up. As in all trapping, you have to get out and do this before you find yourself in a survival situation. Little lessons learned are the key to successful trapping.

Super Stakes

If you're dead set on nailing big-time coyotes, there is a new staking device called super stakes. They are made out of half-inch pipe and are about 4 inches long with 18 inches of cable attached. You have to buy the driving tool to use them, but are they slick. You drive the anchor down 16 or 17 inches, remove the driver and pull up on the anchor at an angle. This forces the anchor to set in the ground at an angle. Let me tell you, when this baby is set, nothing will pull them out. You wire the two cable ends together with two loops of 14-gauge wire or one loop of 11-gauge wire. You can use this stake with leg-hold traps also.

The advantage of this stake system is that it is lightweight, easy to use, and no coyote can pull it out. The disadvantage of this system is that sometimes the driver gets packed with dirt and holds it to the anchor. If this happens, use your hammer to whack the handle back and forth to loosen the dirt and work the driver out. After you are done trapping, the anchor has to be dug out or left for next year. *Don't ever leave these in farmers' fields* as they will tear up their plowing machines and will cost the farmer a lot of money.

Snaring Beavers

Beavers are probably the easiest animals to start with. The beavers have trails everywhere that anyone can understand. Place your snares up on land. Find a good trail that is narrowed down away from the water. Make an 8-inch loop, 10 inches off the ground at the top and 2 inches off the ground on the bottom. You can make the loop larger to keep the small beaver from being caught. Snares are truly selective when you are chasing beaver. Just snare the larger beaver off and leave the smaller ones for next year. This is how you gain food and fur on the long-term plan.

Once snared, the beaver becomes docile in the snare and will just sit, still alive, and wait for you. Shoot him in the head with a .22 short *if it's legal in your state.*

Snaring Beavers Under the Ice

The big secret here is to use $1/16$ snare wire under the ice. Boil the snares in baking soda for 10 minutes, rinse them off and leave them outside until they become dull. Now take a dead branch, 3–4 inches in diameter, and nail it on four pieces of poplar branch, partially peeled, so the white shows.

You have to set this between the feed pile and the den. Chop a hole in the ice, put the stick in and measure the depth you want the top snares—about 4 inches below the surface with a 6 inch loop. Place 2 more snares in the water below those. Nail the bait sticks on either side of the snare so, as the beavers swim around the branch to get the bait, they swim into the snares. Wire the snare tight to the pole and using a small piece of 14 gauge wire. Bend and squeeze it shut to hold each snare at the correct height. Now wire the snares to the pole and run more wire up to a top stick—just in case it is some monster 65 pounder. After you set, leave it alone for 3 days. The beaver can become trap shy by hearing unfamiliar sounds so, just hearing you walk around will sometimes cause them to stay in the den for days.

I could not close my discussion of snaring without mentioning deadfalls using the Figure 4 triggering device. I have been asked many times to comment on them. This is my reply. Back in the late 70s, I made fifty deadfalls for raccoons. The theory behind deadfalls is that the weight (of the logs or stones) has to be 2 to 3 times the weight of the animal. I was trapping raccoons so I figured for a 20 lb. coon, I would need a 60 lb. log. So I made up all these deadfalls with 50 to 60 pound logs. I pre-baited the coons for two weeks before the season opened. Then, when the season opened, I figured I'd nail 6 to 10 coons a day. At $15 each, that was good money for a high school kid. Do you know how many coons I caught in the deadfalls? None! I caught a couple of possums and had a lot of stolen bait. The Figure 4 (or Trigger 4) takes a ton of practice and it is a lot of work to get everything set up. Why would anyone go through all that trouble when you can use real modern equipment?

If I had been using a #220 Conibear instead of deadfalls I would have nailed 6 to 10 coons a night. So, if you want to *play* at trapping then, by all means, make spring pole snares and deadfalls. If you want to feed your family or make money selling fur, then get real equipment. Your time is valuable—why waste it playing with deadfalls and spring pole snares? Look at the time spent. Once you know the basics of modern snaring, you can set one in 5 minutes. How long does it take to build a spring pole snare? An hour or more. You can set a #220 Conibear in 5 minutes. How long does it take to make a deadfall? At least an hour and a half! Now, I'm not talking about someone who has been making these types of traps for years. I'm talking about the average person just starting out.

I guarantee you that if you use modern equipment, follow what I have to say and make the sets like I do, you will catch seven to eight times more animals than you ever could with deadfalls and spring pole snares.

All in all, in addition to using modern equipment, the most important thing you should remember about snares is that they are hard to find so make darn sure you keep track of them. Whether you use surveyor tape or sticks against nearby trees, make sure you know where and how many you set. This is especially important in a survival situation when you can't run to your local dealer to buy more. And, as always, verify your state's particular regulations before venturing out.

Note: All snares in these photos are untreated.

Snare set for coon in Indiana. (This snare could be used for any medium size animal.) The trail naturally went under the stick.

Small snare.

Camlock Snare
1. Camlock
2. Whammy or support collar; the whammy hooks into the #9 wire
3. #9 wire
4. 24" rebar stake

Setting a snare with #9 wire

Hook the driver into the #9 wire, then drive the #9 wire into the ground.

Remove the driver (rebar) and the snare is set. You see why snares are so hard to find.

6 Preparing the Animals

nce you have caught the animals, you have to prepare the pelts for market and clean the animal for cooking. I will first give you a basic overview of proper pelt preparation, which is covered in thorough detail in **Pelt Handling for Profit** produced by Fur Harvesters Auction, Inc. (FHA) of North Bay Ontario, Canada. FHA was generous enough to allow me to include portions of their report in this book. You can also sell your furs through them. After all these years of selling fur, I have found FHA to be the fairest fur dealer I have ever dealt with.

The first thing you want to do after you get back home is to start drying the pelts. If the animals are wet, wrap them in old newspapers. Then, in an hour or so, remove all the mud and dirt by combing the animal from the head down to the tail with a fur comb. (You can get one of these at any trapping supply house.) If the animal is still wet, re-wrap it in fresh newspapers and go to the next animal. Repeat the process with all the animals until they are dry. If one is dry before the others, then you can start skinning him first.

Cased Skinning

Except for beavers, which are skinned open, all animals are skinned cased. Cased skinning is as follows. Make cuts from the two back legs to meet by the tail. You then strip the tailbone out and pull the skin down to the front legs. Cut all the way around the front legs just above the paw. Work the skin down and pull the leg out. Repeat on the other side. Work the skin down, using your knife only when the pelt gets stuck. The pelt is strong and you can pull on it pretty darn hard.

Next, you will come up to the ear cartilage. Take your knife and slice straight down until the ear hole pops up. Do both ears and keep working the skin down. When you are ready to cut the eyes, they will be dark purple and bulging. Make sure you have a sharp knife and slice just in front of the eye. You will see the eyeball clearly at this point. The eyebrows stay on the pelt. Keep carefully cutting in a seesaw motion just in front of the eyes all the way to the nose. The nose is sliced off and stays with the pelt.

Fleshing the Animal

The next step is to flesh the animal. Remove all the fat and muscle off the pelt. Foxes, coyotes, and bobcats can be done with a sharp knife. Muskrats and minks are fairly easy to flesh also. Raccoons, possums, skunks and beavers are the worst.

To flesh, just grab the fat, pull it toward you and slowly cut it off. Be careful not to rip the pelt. Place the skinned pelt on a wooden stretcher and, using a dull tablespoon, press down on the fat and work it down from the top to the bottom, front and back. With that, you are done fleshing.

For beavers, raccoons, opossums, and skunks you will need a fleshing knife and a fleshing beam. A fleshing knife looks like a drawknife, it has a curved blade with a handle on each end. One side is sharp for cutting muscle and gristle, the other side is dull for pushing the fat off.

The fleshing beam is roughly a four to five foot long 1 x 6 or 1 x 8, 1½ inches wide at the upper part. It is tapered 12 inches lengthwise from the upper part to the board width. Each of the four corners is rounded off. Mount the board to the center of a sawhorse. The bottom rests on the floor and the top rests roughly at hip level.

With the raccoons, skunks and opossums, you slide the pelt down on the fleshing beam. Starting at the head, use the sharp end of the fleshing knife to cut the gristle and muscle just below the ears. Slowly work down the pelt. Once you are about 4 inches from the head, flip the fleshing tool over to the dull side and push the fat off. This sounds simple but it takes practice. Wear an apron and lean on the fleshing beam holding the pelt tight. You can place a lot of pressure on the pelt but don't ever allow the pelt to get bunched up or you will rip holes in it.

Finish the back and roll the pelt to the stomach side up. Use the sharp side carefully around the front legs then switch to the dull side and push the fat off. This takes time to do and understand. Don't worry—you will most likely rip a hole in a pelt here and there. We all have done it. Learn from your mistakes.

Skinning Open

Beaver is skinned open. This is how I tell beginners to do it. Cut off all four feet at the first joint then cut off the tail. Take a sharp knife and, with the beaver on its back, make your cut from the center of the chin to the tail. You can use your finger to start from the belly pushing to the chin to lift the fur up. This gives you a line to follow. Make sure you keep the center even.

Once this cut is complete, pull the fur to one side of the beaver and slowly fillet the pelt around that side. Push the legs in and cut the fur back along the leg until you're at the first joint. Then cut the fur so you have a small hole where the leg was. Do this to all four legs and work the pelt all the way around to the back.

On the back, work the pelt off by cutting around from the sides to the tail. Once you have the pelt free from the tail area, work the pelt to the head. Do the head the same way you cased skin, cutting the ear cartilage, the eyes and the nose. Beavers' fat is notorious for dulling knives, so when you're skinning them, have two sharp knifes on hand.

Fleshing beaver is done on the fleshing beam. You place the pelt on the beam with the nose at the front. Using the sharp end of the fleshing knife cut and remove all the flesh and cut the ear cartilage down. Slowly work the muscle down the center of the back until you reach the tail. Place the pelt on its side and work from the clean area down through the muscle with the sharp edge. About half way down, flip to the dull side of the knife and push all the meat and fat off down to the edge. Repeat on the other side. It took me 1½ hours to skin my first beaver. Now, in 45 minutes I can skin, flesh and tack out a beaver. So there is a learning curve involved here. Just think of how it was when you first started your job. Did you do everything perfectly your first day? Of course not!

Wooden Stretchers

Your furs are placed on wooden stretchers while they dry to make sure the furs conform to the proper shape. The stretching board is made out of ½ inch plywood or a 1 x 8 board. The side corners are tapered and sanded smooth, just like a fleshing beam.

Refer to the table on the following page to determine the proper dimensions required for each pelt.

All measurements are in inches:

Animal	Animal Length	Base	Shoulder Width	Tapered to tip
Mink	30	3	2	½
Muskrat	24	7	4	1
Otter	60	7½	5	1
Raccoon	48	8	6	1½
Fox	48	7	5½	1½
Coyote	60	8	6	1¾
Opossum	34	8	5	1
Bobcat	60	8	6	1

Wedge Boards

A wedge board is a small board about two inches wide that tapers to ½ inch. It must be used to keep the pelt from drying too hard on the board. It is placed on the belly side of the fur after the pelt has been placed on the board. Without the wedge board, it is very difficult to remove the dried pelt.

Drying pelts

Most pelts are dry in three to four days. Store them in a cool dark spot away from direct sunlight. The best place is in the basement rafters. Pound nails in the rafters, leaving an inch out for hanging. Then place the fur on the stretcher and hang it from the nails in the rafters. After the pelt is dry, remove it and hang it on a nail until you sell it.

Make sure no mice can get to the pelt or they will chew it up. If there are holes, they should be in the head only. Otherwise, if you have any holes in the pelts, from bullets or a slip with the knife, you must repair them. Use fishing line and a large sewing needle. Do this while the pelt is fresh before you begin stretching it. You'll lose 15-20% for having a sewn pelt but you'll lose 35 to 50% on one with a hole in it. So, you see, you will get docked for a slightly damaged pelt but not as much if you leave the hole open.

Fur prices

The following chart was created from one of my actual bills of sale. It represents my total catches and earnings in one week of trapping. Prices do fluctuate. However, this is a sampling of what can be earned. Not bad for one week!

Beaver

Size	Color	Price
large	Brown to Red—over all	$28.00
X-large	Pale	$17.00
X-large	Clear, very dark natural color	$45.00
X-large	Dark, slightly brownish	$45.00
X-large	Brown to Red—over all	$40.00
X-large	Brown to Red—over all	$40.00
X-large (2)	Dark, slightly brownish	$39.00
X-large (3)	Dark, slightly brownish	$41.00
Large	Dark, slightly brownish	$37.00
Large-Med.	Brown to Red—over all	$13.00
Medium	Dark, slightly brownish	$17.00
Medium	Damaged	$ 4.00
Small	Dark, slightly brownish	$13.00
Small	Damaged	$11.00
Cub	Slightly damaged	$ 5.00
	Total received–Beaver:	$516.00

Muskrat

Size		Price
Average		$1.31
	Total received–Muskrat:	$1.31

Red Foxes

Size	Color	Price
Large	Pale Red	$26.00
Large	Deep, Dark Rich Red	$25.00
Large	Pale Red	$24.00
Large	Pale Red	$24.00
Med/Small	Medium Dark Red	$16.00
Med/Small	Pale Red	$14.00
Med/Small	Medium Dark-Pale Red	$17.00
X-large/Lg.	Pale Red-Very Pale	$26.00
X-large/Lg.	Pale Red-Very Pale	$26.00
	Total received–Red Fox:	$198.00
	Grand Total:	$715.31

The information on the following pages was supplied by trappers for the benefit of trappers. It will cover pelt preparation and handling for beaver, wild mink, raccoon, muskrat, otter and red fox. In addition, it will give you a better feel for the business of trapping and how you can immediately begin making a profit from your catches. I have included portions of this manual because in my opinion, this is the most market driven information a trapper could have.

Fur Harvesters
Pelt Handling for Profit

FUR HARVESTERS AUCTION INC.

PELT HANDLING FOR PROFIT
$ $ $

Source: Pelt Handling for Profit, Fur Harvesters of North Bay, Ontario, Canada, Auction, Inc.
©1999, Fur Harvesters Auction, Inc. Reproduced with permission.

BROTHERS OF THE HARVEST

Each face represents the traditional image of the Native and Non-native fur harvester. The Beaver is the hardest and most persistent worker in the world. The Beaver has also been traditionally the back bone of the fur industry. The maple leaf reflects the Canadian heritage of this industry. The two circles that surround the inner images is the creator. He is within you and around you. The two circles are also connected by small lines that represent our own connection with the Creator, as well as a skin that is stretched out, an image well known in the fur industry.

MARKETING YOUR WILD FUR

Today, trappers have many options for marketing their pelts. If you are considering shipping to an international auction house, Fur Harvesters Auction Inc. (FHA) is the logical choice.

This year, FHA has planned four (4) sales, three (3) in North Bay and one (I) in Seattle. FHA is recognized around the world for its fine collections of wild fur. To ensure these sales are well attended by both North American and overseas buyers, FHA representatives have made several soliciting trips to promote its product. At our sale in Seattle, your pelts will be sold along side the finest ranch mink collection in the world. With Seattle's proximity to the Orient, this sale will target this very important emerging market.

CONDITIONS OF SALE

I. FHA's sales commission is II%.
2. There are shipping costs for using FHA's pick up services. Please check your appropriate schedule for the applicable amounts.
3. FHA will sell your pelts at its discretion. As always, FHA will continue to protect your interests and obtain the best prices possible for your fur.
4. If not previously paid, royalties will be deducted and remitted to the province in question.
5. Your fur shipment is fully insured by FHA when your agent issues you a receipt. Your shipment is also insured if you ship directly to FHA by a common (registered) carrier.
6. FHA's sales our conducted in U.S. dollars. If you are a Canadian shipper, your proceeds will be converted and paid to you in Canadian funds.
7. Unsold goods are not returnable. They will be re-offered on subsequent sales until sold.
8. Drumming charges will be deducted for all long hair pelts that are drummed. Drumming cleans and improves the appearance of the long haired pelts and increases their value.
9. A shrinkage allowance is calculated on all castoreum shipments. The amount of this allowance is at FHA's discretion.

PELT HANDLING FOR PROFIT
1999 Edition

BEAVER PELT HANDLING

REMOVING BEAVERS FROM TRAPS

Beaver should be removed from traps carefully, so not to damage the pelt. When trapping in winter, extra care must be taken. Remove the beaver from the trap as soon as it is out of the water, so it does not freeze to the metal. Be especially cautious where the water is shallow and the fur may have frozen to the ice. If the beaver should become frozen in the trap, allow it to thaw before attempting removal. Never put a wet animal on or against anything to which it might freeze.

If the fur is dirty, wash the beaver in water. In winter, rub the animal in loose snow to clean and dry it. The snow will absorb extra moisture so that the fur does not freeze. Next, it is best to place the beaver in a burlap or feed type bag. This will prevent it from freezing to your truck or the type of equipment you are using.

SKINNING THE BEAVER

Skinning the "open" pelt is much different than skinning the "cased" pelt. By this method, the animal is laid on its back on a clean place. With the beaver, the feet and tail are first cut off.

Cutting these parts from the beaver is not difficult but there is an easy way. On the tail at the first fringe of fur, there is a flat joint. This joint is about 1/4 inch into the fringe of fur. A little practice will make this joint easy to find and the tail can be cut off with one slice of the knife across the flat joint. Very close to the fringe of fur above the feet on the front legs is another joint. This joint can be felt with the finger and thumb and one cut across the joint with a sharp knife will sever the foot.

To cut off the hind foot, first, bend the foot forward towards the belly of the beaver, bending it fully forward at the heel. With the foot held this way, cut across the cords at the back of the foot and keep cutting all around the foot with it still bent forward. A snap sideways after this cut is finished will usually break the foot free from the leg.

The next step is to slit the pelt from the chin to the tail on the belly side and in a straight line (see Figure 1). The pelt is then skinned back one side at a time to the back. When the legs are reached, do not slit them open but pull them

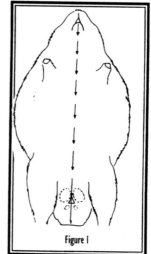

Figure 1

PELT HANDLING FOR PROFIT
1999 Edition

through, pulling the hide off the way you would take off a sock. Be careful with the skinning knife around the legs because the skin is easily cut in these tender places. Skin carefully the head. Cut the ears off close to the skull. Skin around the eyes and nose and the pelt is free from the carcass.

Note: Beaver castors, on both male and female, are found on each side and just forward of the vent. These should be removed carefully with a knife or pulled free with the thumb and finger so the sacks are not broken, which would let the oil run out. They should be tied at the cords and hung until dry. The more care used in removing and drying, the more castors are worth. They are used in making scents and perfumes.

THE DRYING BOARD

The drying boards are made from a single sheet of 4'x8'x3/4" plywood. Cut the sheet into three pieces measuring 32"x48". The drying board should be marked as shown. This is done on both sides of the board, giving you six stretching surfaces from one sheet of plywood.

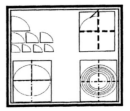

The pattern templates are available at no cost at Fur Harvesters Auction. Choose the line appropriate to the length of the pelt, and fasten the head and tail to the drying board with the fur side down. The nails which are used to attach the pelt should extend at least 1" above the pelt so that when the nailing of the pelt is complete, it can be raised off the board. This allows the air to circulate between the fur and the board (2" common nails work well). Place one nail behind the nose and one at the tail, and one at the mid-length on each side of the pelt.

IMPORTANT!! The lines on the board should only be used as a guide to give you a consistent uniform shape. Using a tape measure, measure from the nail at the nose to the tail. Add this to the width measurement. The sum of the two will give you your GREEN size. Refer to size chart:

SIZING OVAL SHAPE

0	XXXL:	Supers over 70"
1	XXL:	65" to 70"
2	XL:	60" to 65"
3	LGE:	55" to 60"
4	LM:	51" to 55"
5	MED:	47" to 51"
6	SMALL:	42" to 47"
7	CUB:	Under 42"

PELT HANDLING FOR PROFIT
1999 Edition

A beaver pelt will almost always shrink approximately 2" from the time you board it until you take it off. If the skin measures 61" GREEN, it is an XL, but when it is dry it will most likely be a large size approximately 59" putting it down one size, at the upper limit of the large size tariff.

This is where the trapper <u>makes or loses</u> money depending on how he or she boards the pelt. Always board the pelt 2" to 3" above the size tariff suited to the size of the pelt. The skin boarded at 61" GREEN, if it can be boarded 2" larger and *still remain loose* on the board would remain in the XL category. Two beaver of exactly the same quality when boarded differently can easily sell for a $5 - $10 difference.

Always remember a freshly boarded beaver will almost always shrink 2 to 3 inches during the drying process. Both pelts will fall into the large category but the grade of the two could be quite different. An example of this based on December 1995's sale would be as follows:

SHEARABLE GRADES:

Size 3 (LGE) IPTII B	$40.00
Size 3 (LGE) I&II HVY B	$34.00
Size 3 (LGE)I-II SEMI B	$24.00

NON-SHEARABLE GRADES:

Size 3 (LGE) I-II FLAT B	$17.00

The 56 inch beaver will have a far better chance of falling into one of the shearable grades as would the one at 59 inches. By boarding your beaver pelts properly, the trapper will be getting the best quality grade possible. *YOU WILL RECEIVE FAR MORE SHEARABLE GRADES BY BOARDING YOUR BEAVER LOOSELY, THAN THE PERSON WHO STRETCHES IT TIGHT. HE MAY GAIN IN SIZE, BUT THE MARKET IS DEMANDING A SHEARABLE PRODUCT.*

Once you have determined your size, continue to nail the top half of the pelt to the board. Space the nails about 3/4" apart. When the top half is completed, continue to place nails at the same intervals along the bottom half of the pelt, until it has an even sided shape that follows the pattern on the board. This will help prevent over stretching which reduces the density of the fur and lessens its value.

The leg holes should not be left open because they give the pelt a rough appearance. It is preferred to sew the leg holes, but

PELT HANDLING FOR PROFIT
1999 Edition

nailing them closed is also acceptable. After the leg holes have been closed, wash the leather lightly with water and some paper towel or cloth. This will remove blood stains and light grease. The leather will take on a creamy whitish appearance. Next, lift the pelt up off the nails so the air can circulate under the skin. *Many trappers who use boards prefer to do their fleshing after the pelt has been tacked to the board. This should be done before the leg holes are closed.*

DRYING

It is best to dry beaver pelts slowly. Temperatures of $55^0 - 65^0$ F are desirable. Never put drying pelts near stoves or expose them to hot sunlight. As the pelt dries, wipe the leather from time to time with a clean cloth. This removes any grease which may run from the leather.

MARKETING THE BEAVER

Over the years, more black spots have been showing up on the beaver. These marks are most often old scars. Old scars that are hard and brittle must be classified as slight damage. The reason for that is when they go into the tanning fluid, it will not penetrate the hard scars and when the knife used to thin the leather hits these scars, the pelt can be damaged.

1.	I PT II A	SELECT		16.	REG SLT DGD A	NON- SHEARABLE -
2.	I PT II B	SHEARABLE		17.	REG SLT DGD B	SLT CUTS, SCARS
3.	I PT II C			18.	REG SLT DGD C	
4.	I-II HVY A			19.	I-II RED RUMP B	VERY FLAT, TAKEN
5.	I-II HVY B			20.	I-II RED RUMP C	VERY EARLY, BLUE
6.	I-II HVY C	SHEARABLE		21.	GOOD II'S B	LEATHER
7.	I-II SEMI A			22.	GOOD II'C	
8.	I-II SEMI B					
9.	I-II SEMI C			23.	GOOD DAMAGED	CUTS, BITES 30% PELT DGD
				24.	III'S & IV'S UNPRIME OR SICK	
10.	I-II FLAT A	NON-SHEARABLE		25.	BDLY DGD MANY CUTS OR HOLES OVER 30% DGD	
11.	I-II FLAT B					
12.	I-II FLAT C					
13.	GOOD SLT DGD A	SHEARABLE - SLT				
14.	GOOD SLT DGD B	CUTS, SCARS				
15.	GOOD SLT DGD C					

PELT HANDLING FOR PROFIT
1999 Edition

There are very few select pelts. A grade pattern is established primarily because all the pelts are intersorted. If you have a pelt worth $50 you would not expect it to be put with pelts worth $40, as the maximum you would realize would be $40. This is what necessitates fine grading.

PRIMENESS IN BEAVER

The underfur of the beaver is almost absent in the summer. However, towards fall, these hairs start to grow. The last place on the animal where they finish growing is the back of the neck. In the fall, they are quite short. However a full prime skin will have hair on the back of the neck, approximately 3/4" long. This is why when grading, the back of the neck is felt. The amount of resistance the hand feels in rubbing the beaver against the grain of the fur, indicates the density of the underfur. When it is very flat, it is called a II or III. As it comes into prime, the hair thickens and it can be classified as I PT II or I-II, depending on how thick the fur grows. Once the full length of the hair has been reached, the fur and pelt start to become over-prime. The beaver, because of its long stay in the house and sour feed source, has been using its body fat to produce fur and keep warm. As this progresses, the underfur starts to turn "off" colour or reddish. This occurs in a spring beaver and is referred to as red rump. It starts at the tail and progresses up the flanks, rendering the beaver useless for plucking and shearing, because the red stain goes below the 12mm level. This is the reason fall beaver pelts are much more desirable than spring pelts.

If your beaver pelts are sent to Fur Harvesters Auction and they are consistently graded I-II HVY, I-II SEMI on your returns, your handling is satisfactory.

Not satisfied?? Ask... at a trapper education course or at our annual convention. Ask someone you know who does a top job and they will be glad to share their knowledge. Time, practice and interest make the finest fur handlers.

103

WILD MINK PELT HANDLING

PREPARING THE MINK FOR PELTING

The very first step, as with any pelt handling, is to have a clean, dry mink, free of mud, burrs and dirt. If your mink is completely dry, one must pay attention to singe. Lightly dampen the pelt before removing it from the carcass. The best method is a spray bottle. Adjust the spray to a fine mist. Do not soak the pelt, but rather dampen the pelt until it is moist when touched.

SKINNING THE MINK

Begin by removing the front legs. This makes the job easier when trying to pull the pelt free later on. Next, cut from one back leg to the other (Figure I). The cut is on the belly side of the vent hole. Place the one leg in some form of holding device and pull on the other leg. You will notice a natural line follows across from paw to paw. By using this method, the fur harvester gains two things: increased length and the inspection area is enhanced. Both help improve the price paid.

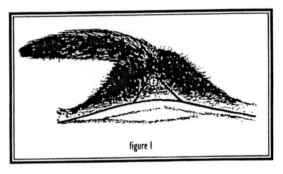

figure I

Remove the tail bone using a tail stripper. Proceed to pull the pelt down towards the front legs. If the mink is a male, you must remove the penis bone. After pulling the pelt down to the front legs, work your fingers between the leg and body. Pull the leg through. When the front paws are already removed, this step is much easier. Finally, pull the pelt clear of the carcass using a knife to cut the ears, eyes, and nose clear.

BOARDING

The next step in this process is boarding. This is another important step. Use a female board for females and a male board for males. If you put males on female boards and try to get all extra large skins, you will be down graded to a

PELT HANDLING FOR PROFIT
1999 Edition

smaller size or two. We strongly recommend a solid one piece board.

Before pinning the pelt with 5/8" push pins, the pelt must be fleshed of fat and grease. Place the pelt on the board with each hind leg on opposite sides of the board. Remove fat from front leg area with a dull knife scraping the fat forward toward the leg hole. **Do not remove the red saddle.** The saddle on mink protects the skin from over scraping which can cause root hair damage. At auction, a mink with the saddle removed usually brings $2 to $3 less than mink with the saddle on. If the saddle has excess fat under it, gently scrape the saddle pushing the grease and oil out.

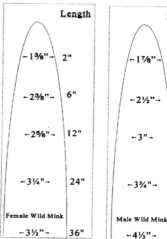

Female Wild Mink		Male Wild Mink	
	Length		Length
←1⅝"→ 2"		←1⅞"→ 2"	
←2⅜"→ 6"		←2½"→ 6"	
←2⅝"→ 12"		←3"→ 12"	
←3¼"→ 24"		←3¾"→ 24"	
←3½"→ 36"		←4½"→ 36"	

Next, turn the pelt so the legs are opposite the tail. Make sure the pelt is straight on the board. TIP: Place the length measurement for the mink on your boards. This way, you know what size pelt you are working with.

SIZING

MALES   ### FEMALES

MALES			FEMALES		
XXL	=	Over 23"	XL	=	Over 19"
XL	=	21" - 23"	LGE	=	17" - 19"
LGE	=	19" - 21"	M&S	=	Under 17"
LM	=	17" - 19"			
M&S	=	under 17"			

Scrape the fat and grease from the belly area. Remember to wipe the fur clean of any excess oil with a paper towel. *Mink pelts can singe so be careful.*

PELT HANDLING FOR PROFIT
1999 Edition

Follow that by pinning the hind legs on the back of the board with the tail. Check the board measurement with the pelt, match the best line with the pelt size. Begin pinning the tail in a slight pleating method. *What you want to do is push as much fur into the inspection area as possible (Figure 2).* You can use push pins, wire mesh, cardboard or whatever works best for you.

Cut a piece of fur out of the belly side to enhance the inspection area. Next, tuck the front legs inside the pelt. Remove the lower lip. This helps the auction house attach your identification ticket to the pelt.

Finally, hang the pelt up with nose down allowing the oil to run down toward the head. Allow two to three days at 50^0-60^0F for drying. Remove from board and store in a cool dry place until shipping. When marketing mink, the earlier the better is the general rule. Most years, the best prices are on the first and second sales. After that, the price drops quickly.

Figure 2

RACCOON PELT HANDLING

REMOVAL FROM TRAP

When taking the animal out of the trap, avoid removing any of the fur. Thorough waxing of the traps should prevent such problems. If the raccoon should become frozen in the trap, allow it to thaw in a warm place before attempting to remove it.

PREPARATION OF SKINNING

Before skinning, the animal should be clean, combed and dry. If wet or muddy, hang by front feet in front of a fan using no heat and combing every hour or so.

SKINNING THE RACCOON

Because of the fat, it is often easier to rough skin and flesh afterwards. Start skinning by slitting down from the heel of each hind paw. The cut should pass 5 cm (2 inches) below the vent. See Figure I. This is the most important cut, sometimes called the money cut.

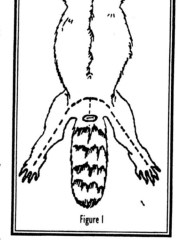

Figure I

Then strip the tail by pulling downward. On big raccoons, it may be necessary to split the tail part way down. Use a tail stripper. Ring cut the front legs at elbow joint. Skin down the front legs and cut the fur free. Skin carefully around the neck and cut the ears close to the skull. Continue down, cutting around the eyes, lips and nose, until the pelt becomes free. Leave the bottom chin lip on the carcass.

FLESHING AND DRYING

Pelt should be cool before attempting to flesh.

PELT HANDLING FOR PROFIT
1999 Edition

Pull the pelt onto the fleshing beam and scrape until all the fat and flesh is removed. It is especially important to scrape all gristle from the ears and the back of the neck. Do not over scrape. Try to keep the grease off the fur during fleshing. The toughest part of fleshing a raccoon is the neck. Sometimes, scoring the gristle with a knife, just below the ears, will help you get started.

To soak up grease, some trappers use a dry, fine sawdust which contains no resin.

The tail must be split and fleshed!!!

Sew or push pin shut holes that appear in pelt. Care should be taken not to over scrape pelts, especially early blue pelts where the hair roots can be damaged.

Wipe the fleshed pelt with a dry cloth. Make sure the fur is completely dry before placing it on a standard drying board.

STRETCHING RACCOON

Clean wire frames and board (no split boards) are both suitable for drying raccoon.

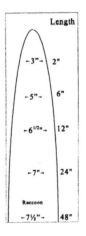

Depending on the fur section you come from, northern heavy type raccoon, NY, Wisconsin, Michigan, Minnesota, Iowa look good on wood boards, semi heavy and coat type look better on wire stretchers. Smaller size and northern raccoon also will look better on wire. Make sure the pelt is centred properly on the stretcher. All Raccoon should be put up leather out. Raccoon are marketed leather out.

CUTTING THE WINDOW

On a male, cut the window up to the penis hole. On a female, cut the window to the lower two teats. Keep your window narrow, the flanks are very important when the manufacturers make the garments. If the window is made too wide, it can hurt the value of the pelt. Window should be made right after the pelt is put on the stretcher, never once the pelt is dry.

PELT HANDLING FOR PROFIT
1999 Edition

SIZING

XXXL	=	Over 32"
XXL	=	29" - 32"
XL	=	27" - 29"
LGE	=	24" - 27"
LM	=	22" - 24"
M&S	=	Under 22"

TAKING THE RACCOON OFF STRETCHER

1. Wipe racoon first with rag or paper towel to remove excess wet grease.

2. Remove pelt from stretcher and comb out inspection area.

STORAGE - BEFORE SHIPPING

1. Put in FHA fur bag, head first. Store in cool, dark, dry place.

Be on the lookout for things such as mice, squirrels, fur bugs that like to eat fur.

PELT HANDLING FOR PROFIT
1999 Edition

MUSKRAT PELT HANDLING

PREPARING THE MUSKRAT FOR SKINNING

Muskrat should not be removed from frozen traps. If the muskrat is frozen in the trap, thaw the trap and rat first before removing the animal. This can be accomplished by submerging the rat and trap in water or by hanging the trap and rat in your fur shed at room temperature.

Before skinning, the muskrat must be completely dry.

PELTING PROCEDURE

Pelting should be done with a long, thin, sharply pointed blade approximately 3.5" to 4" in length.

The pelt must be dried and combed before proceeding. However, if skinning is done on the trapline and you intend to board it later, the pelt should be turned with the fur out and rolled for transportation. Later in your home or shed, it must be hung until dried and cooled before fleshing.

SKINNING

Prepare to skin by either laying the muskrat on its back or by hanging it from its tail from over head, with its tail nearest your knife hand. Grasp the right foot and make a straight cut from the base of the heel to the tail. Continue to push the knife through the underside of the tail and cut up leaving 1" to 11/2" of tail attached to the belly fur (See figure 1). Turn the muskrat around and repeat procedure meeting at tail incision. You will notice the line where the fur from the back (longer) meets the belly fur (shorter).

The 1" to 11/2" of tail left on the skirt of the belly prevents the pelt from tearing when it is mounted on the wire stretcher. Free the back side of the muskrat leaving the same amount of tail skin as done on the underside.

Now, with these cuts completed, work your hand up the back between the pelt and the flesh. Work the pelt over the head, cutting the ears close to the skull and with care around eyes and mouth. Next pull the front feet through the pelt and carefully work the pelt away from the belly down to the tail flap.

PELT HANDLING FOR PROFIT
1999 Edition

FLESHING AND STRETCHING THE MUSKRAT

Excess fat and meat should only be removed. ***The saddle must be left on.*** Removal of the saddle will leave your rats papery and have less value. We recommend using wire stretchers as it gives each muskrat at proper fit. However, wooden stretchers are and can be used.

As with all pelts, make sure the pelt is centred properly on the stretcher. Pull the pelt down snugly on the wire frame. Insert the tension hooks into the tail leather. This eliminates the chance of ripping the thin belly leather. Make sure the nose does not slip over the end of the stretcher. Use a clothes pin or a nail through the nose.

Wipe off excess grease with paper towel or cloth.

Figure 1

111

PELT HANDLING FOR PROFIT
1999 Edition

OTTER PELT HANDLING

Most fur harvesters find the otter one of the most difficult furbearers to handle. We will cover pelting and handling tips which will make handling this important fur easier and more profitable for you.

To start with, as with any type of fur harvesting, the tools we use must be humane and the system of using the tools must also be humane. The otter is probably the strongest and toughest aquatic animal. Conibears of the 220 or 280 size, dyed and waxed are good methods. Smaller or larger sizes of conibear are either too weak or too slow. Even setting beaver dams that are active with beaver, it is much better to use a 280 conibear, instead of a 330 conibear. The 330 conibear while an excellent beaver trap, is too large to be effective for otter that are usually present in the water system. Other methods of harvesting are by using leg holds of the 3 or 4 size in a drowning slide wire system or snaring. With snaring, we must stress the importance of making sure not to snare otter on dry land. This technique is to be used under the ice. Snaring otter on dry land causes damage and is not a humane method of harvesting.

The first step in handling an otter is to have the proper equipment. The basic tools required are a sharp skinning knife, a draw knife, fleshing beam, skinning gamble, 5/8" push pins, water bottle with a spray nozzle, a fur comb and a sharp pair of scissors along with clean saw dust and paper towels.

The most common grades that a fur harvester sees on his fur cheque are singed and straight hair. We all want to have straight hair otter but most of us end up with singed otter. Singe is a form of hair damage. It occurs naturally in otter that are harvested late in the season. Singe also occurs in the handling of otter after you harvest the furbearer. Most otter start out as straight hair and end up being singed.

The first step in avoiding singe begins out on your trap line. <u>Make sure to keep the otter wet, clean and out of the heat. Place the otter in a clean canvas or burlap bag. Do not allow it to freeze to the boat or vehicle you are using. The next problem one can encounter is placing the otter too close to heat. Be careful not to place the otter too close to the heater in your vehicle or to thaw in front of the wood stove. Both of these can cause singe on the otter.</u>

PELTING

Begin by wetting down the otter with water using the spray bottle. Wet the otter from head to tail with a light spray. Avoid skinning the otter when it is completely dry. After wetting the fur, brush from head to tail removing any dirt or mats.

PELT HANDLING FOR PROFIT
1999 Edition

Place otter on skinning gamble. Using a sharp knife, cut from hind foot to tail side of vent hole, repeat for other leg . Next, cut around both front legs to make it easier. Next, cut from bottom of vent hole to tip of tail. Using your knife, carefully cut out the tail. Once you have the base of the tail free, you will be able to pull the tail free of the pelt. You must be very careful not to get grease on the pelt.

Continue to skin the pelt down towards the front legs. When pulling the pelt from the carcass, allow the saddle and fat to stay on the pelt. Pull front legs through holes already cut in pelt. Pull pelt forward until you reach the ear cartilage. Carefully cut ears close to head. Continue to skin until free of carcass.

Once the rough skinning is complete, place the otter on the fleshing beam. Ensure that the fleshing beam is lightly sprayed with water. Slide pelt completely down on the beam and lightly cover with sawdust. Using a sharp knife, cut the saddle around the head. Next, using the draw knife, begin fleshing the saddle towards the tail. As the saddle peels off, cut the larger pieces off with your skinning knife.

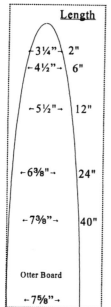

You will find that the fatter the otter, the easier it is to flesh. As you near the tail, be careful to trim off any saddle or fat, using paper towels to clean up any grease. When fleshing, be careful around the belly area. You will find the tail section difficult to flesh using your draw knife, therefore, use your skinning knife carefully to finish off the tail. Once the fleshing is completed, clean off any excess grease using paper towels.

BOARDING

The next step in the handling process is the boarding. Again, we strongly recommend the use of a solid board. Make sure you use a belly wedge. Place otter, fur in, on the board. Centre the pelt on the board making sure the tail is opposite the front legs. Push the head completely to the top of the board. Gently tap the board until the pelt is snug. Begin pinning the tail on board. Pin tail short and wide using a plaiting method. Push as much fur into the inspection area as possible . Now pin the back legs onto the tail side of the board.

The next step is to trim the belly area with your skinning knife. By pinning your otter in this method, the inspection area will already be formed and by trimming the area

PELT HANDLING FOR PROFIT
1999 Edition

you will have a perfect vent. Next, sew the front legs closed. Ensure that the legs are opposite the tail.

The next step is to cut off the lower lip. This is important when you are shipping to the auction house. This is where the ticket identifying your pelt is placed.

Finally, insert the belly wedge and allow to dry for three (3) or four (4) days at a temperature of 50° to 60°F. Every second day, wipe off excess grease and oil from the pelt. After the pelt has dried, remove from the board. Be careful not to run your hand over the inspection area. This can cause otter to singe. If you are not shipping the pelt to market, store in a cool dry place or even better, in your freezer until you are going to ship.

Remember to place the length measurement for the otters on your boards. This way, you know what size pelt you are working with.

SIZING

XL	=	Over 38"
LGE	=	34" - 38"
LM	=	32" - 34"
M&S	=	28" - 32"
XSML	=	Under 28"

By following these simple steps, you will find otter easier to prepare, and you will receive higher returns for your otter pelts.

PELT HANDLING FOR PROFIT
1999 Edition

RED FOX PELT HANDLING

While most fur harvesters do a good job of putting up their red fox, a surprising number of them use boards that are the wrong size.

In today's marketplace, a wise fur producer uses every advantage available to maximize their bottom line. The techniques we are presenting in this article will help you to improve your finished product by increasing fur density, ensuring the largest size is attained and by giving a more uniform finish.

In the wild fur business, fur comes into the auction house in every size and shape under the sun. This causes problems for both the graders and buyers. Because there is so much variation in the size, the fur harvester loses out.

The first step in handling your fox is to have the proper equipment. You need to have a proper skinning knife, draw knife, fleshing beam, skinning gamble, push pins (5/8" size), drying board, lots of sawdust, paper towels, a good fur comb and a tail stripper.

IMPORTANT NOTE: Fox are known rabies carriers, therefore always use surgical gloves. Wash hands and equipment in warm soap and disinfectant after working on a fox. Never skin any animal that you even think was sick.

The equipment you use in the field should be in top condition and well prepared . Check your foot holds and snares for correct working action. Our recommendation when snaring fox is to only use camlocks or power snares where legal. Other locking devices can be used but we feel the camlock and power snares to be the most humane killing tools. In some areas where the use of snares is prohibited, foot hold traps are the most effective to use. Make sure that you use the right size trap. In more urban areas, make sure to use soft catches or foot snares in case of non-target animal captures. Any fox trapper who knows his fox will insist upon a clean, dyed and waxed trap or snare.

A WAXED TRAP IS MUCH MORE EFFECTIVE THAN A RUSTY ONE

When trapping in adverse weather conditions, the fur harvester needs every advantage he/she can use. After removing the fox from your set, care must be used in storage. Place in a clean canvas or burlap bag free of grease and dirt. Pelt fur as quickly as possible. Caution: do not attempt to pelt a frozen or partially frozen fox.

PELT HANDLING FOR PROFIT
1999 Edition

PELTING

The first step in pelting your fur is to brush from head to tip of tail. Remove any dirt or mats as completely as possible. Do not attempt to cut out mats. Next, lay fox on table and grasp front paw and cut from paw to elbow joint in a straight line. The next step is to cut from hind leg to belly side of vent hole. Cut from paw to vent hole using the natural fur line, white and red colour of the fur. Cut completely around the vent. By using your fingers, work around each leg separating the hide. Place fox in a skinning gamble. By using an adjustable set up, one can raise and lower the fox to whatever level is required. A good set up helps save on back pain and increases production.

Using a tail stripper, free the tail from the tail bone. Begin working the pelt forward toward the front legs. Ensure that when skinning a male fox that the penis bone is cut out. When you have worked the pelt all the way down to the front legs, again use your fingers to pull the pelt free of the front legs. Using your knife, ring around the front paws when you have freed them from the pelt.

Pull pelt down toward head. Ensure your knife is sharp. Carefully cut the ear cartilage at the head. Gently pull pelt forward toward the eyes, again cutting close to the head. Finally, cut the nose and bottom lip off the pelt. If pelt is bloody or dirty, wash it in cold water and mild soap. Remove excess water before boarding.

BOARDING:

To start with, we recommend the use of only one size board. The board must be 60" long and 5.25" wide, gently tapered from shoulders to nose. The use of a properly sized board is of great importance for a uniform overall finish. The proper size board for fox will enhance the density of the fur and increase the length of the pelts.

The biggest problem at the auction house is the varying width of the pelts coming to market. Some fur harvesters use boards as wide as racing paddles. The pelt has been improperly stretched. The buyers do not want pelts in a lot that do not look like they fit in with the rest of them.

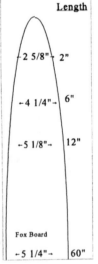

The problem with a split board is that when you open it up at the bottom, you are thinning out the fur on the flanks. Also, length is lost because you are forcing the fur wider and back up towards the

PELT HANDLING FOR PROFIT
1999 Edition

head. The problem with wire stretchers is that some fur harvesters turn the fox before it is dry. When the fox is turned around, the wet skin comes in contact with the metal causing hair slip. Also, the fur harvester cannot pin the fox properly.

The first step in boarding your fox is to place the pelt on the stretcher, fur in. Centre the eyes and ears on the board in line with the tail. Gently tap the bottom of the board on the floor to push the nose and head as far down the board as possible. If the fox is excessively fatty, you will have to flesh it on a beam before placing on the stretcher. Be very careful when beaming a fox as the pelt is not as tough as that of a raccoon or beaver pelt. Be sure to use plenty of sawdust to absorb the grease and fat.

Next, split the tail from the base to the tip using a tail splitting guide and a sharp knife. Pin the tail down using 5/8" push pins.

The third step is to carefully remove the ear cartilage from the ears. You may find this difficult the first few times you do it. The key to removing the cartilage is to make sure you have a good sharp knife and that the fox is fresh. Using the knife, start removing the cartilage. After you have it started, you can work it out with your finger. When finished, you should have a complete ear. Pin the ears on the board toward the eyes. By removing the cartilage, the fur harvesters can prevent hair slip on the ears and head. Be sure to sew any holes or tears when you are boarding the fox.

Next, pin the front and rear legs opposite the tail. Pin legs wide and short. Use sixteen (16) pins per hind leg and about (10) pins per front leg. In order to pin out front legs, you will have to make small stretchers or you can use squirrel stretchers.

Finally, cut the lower lip off of the pelt. Make sure the pelt is centred on the board and the legs are opposite the tail. Use a small belly wedge to help in turning the pelt. Give the edges of the fox a quick brushing to separate the fur from the leather. Allow pelt to dry for 24 hours at a temperature between 50^0- 60 °F. Do not over dry or use excessive heat.

After the pelt has dried, turn the pelt fur out. Be careful to centre the pelt on the board. Leave front legs inside with the skin. Pin tail and hind legs on board. Allow to dry for another two (2) to three (3) days at a temperature of 50^0- 60^0F. Carefully brush fox from head to tip of tail when you first turn pelt and once again when you remove it from the board.

PELT HANDLING FOR PROFIT
1999 Edition

When shipping your fox pelts, please ensure all claws are removed. Ship in a flat position. Do not ship between furs that are fur in, as the grease will damage the fur of your fox pelts.

SIZING

XL	=	Over 32"
LGE	=	29" - 32"
M&S	=	Under 29"

Measurement is from the nose to the base of the tail. By placing the measurements on your boards, the fur harvester knows immediately the size of the fox pelt he/she is working with.

IN SUMMARY

Fur harvesters can increase profit by following these simple steps. By using uniform boards, everyone can benefit and achieve a higher return for their work.

PELT HANDLING FOR PROFIT
1999 Edition

GENERAL FUR HANDLING TIPS

PELT SIZES

While it is never wise to over-stretch fur, there are times when pelts will be on the borderline between two sizes when they are placed on the board. Pelts shrink slightly in length during drying, so it may be to the trapper's advantage to stretch these borderline pelts just a little more to bring them up to the next largest size. To accommodate this, having the pelt sizes marked on your boards for each species may be helpful.

FUR HANDLING AND MARKETING

Proper fur handling and orderly marketing mean dollars in trappers' pockets. Specific pelting procedures for each furbearer are covered in the sections pertaining to those furbearers, but there are important points that are common to all furbearers. Proper fur handling commences with setting the proper traps for each species to ensure clean captures and minimal damage.

REMOVAL FROM TRAPS

Care should be taken when removing animals from traps especially if they are frozen. Simply prying an animal out of a trap may remove portions of fur and down grade pelts. If furbearers are completely frozen in traps, it would be wise to take the furbearer still in the trap to your camp or fur shed and remove it after it has thawed.

TRANSPORTING

Furbearers should be transported in clean burlap or nylon bags (eg. feed sacks) to ensure that they remain clean and that blood or dirt from one animal is not transferred to another. Never place wet furbearers directly onto metal racks of ATV's or snowmobiles or the box of a pickup truck in freezing weather. They will become badly frozen on and difficult to remove without doing major damage to the fur.

CLEANING/STORAGE

In general, ideally furbearers should dry before pelting. Furbearers should be brushed lightly before pelting to remove burrs, mats and dirt, which may stain the fur, and cause cuts in the pelting process. If animals are badly soiled, they should be washed lightly with clean water and allowed to dry before pelting commences. If you cannot skin animals shortly after harvesting, or if you choose to rough skin pelts and flesh at a later date, they should be frozen to preserve quality. Place furbearers or pelts in plastic bags and remove as much air as possible. Tie tightly and place in a freezer. Pelts that are to be frozen should be rolled nose to tail, leather in. Thaw slowly to prevent hair slip before pelting or fleshing. After fleshing and drying, pelts should be shipped to market as soon as possible. If you must store pelts for long periods they should be placed in a freezer. For short periods of storage, keep in a dark, cool dry room. Pelts may be wrapped lightly in newsprint, stored in burlap or nylon bags or hung from hooks or rafters. Ship to market in clean bags or cardboard boxes, never in plastic bags.

PELT HANDLING FOR PROFIT
1999 Edition

EASE OF SHIPPING

- FHA's network of agents are strategically located throughout the United States and Canada.
- Our Agents will ensure your fur is delivered to North Bay safely and as economically as possible.
- All paperwork needed to cross borders are done by the agent.
- Your fur is insured by FHA.
- Many of our agents offer fur pick-up services.
- Please see the next page for your closest agent.

PELT HANDLING FOR PROFIT
1999 Edition

** USA AGENTS **

DAD'S FUR COMPANY
Box 295, Davis Street
Brownville Jct., ME 04415
(207) 965-3057 *Abe & Troy Chase
(207) 965-8881 *Denny Larson

HARVEY DREWELOW
c/o North Iowa Fur Co.
121 North Washington
Fredericksburg, IA 50630
(319) 237-5332

UPPER PENINSULA
TRAPPERS ASSOCIATION
Dan Harrington
w 9402 Peterson Drive
Iron Mountain, MI 49801
(906) 774-3571

THE TRAPPER HAVEN
John Coakley
1188 Turkey Knob Rd.
Quickburg, VA 22847
(540) 477-3440

RICK HEMSATH
c/o Northeast Iowa Fur Co.
Box 96
Rowley, IA 52329
(319) 938-2665

MARK SPENCER
626 Worth Road
Moran, MI 49760
(906) 292-4779

PETER M. TROMBLEE
Route 9, Box 43
Lewis, NY 12950
(518) 873-2622

GARY RUTHERFORD
HCI Box 1749
West Bay Drive
Pengilly, MN 55775
(218) 885-1677

SEATTLE FUR EXCHANGE
200 SW 34th Street
Renton, WA 98055
(425) 251-3100

BILL THOMPSON
PO Box 55
Athens, ME 04912
(207) 654-3576

DAVE WALLACE
Box 148, 505 Kila Rd.
Kila, MT 59920
(406) 257-8823

DAVE DAY
RR 2, Box 2185
Cabot, VT 05647
(802) 563-2667

TOBY EDWARDS
388 Tennantville Road
Edinburg, NY 12134
(518) 863-6716

LARRY RUNNIGEN
410 East Hampden Avenue
Fergus Falls, MN 56537
(218) 736-4208

JIM GRIFFITH
Road 3, Box 111
Stoystown, PA 15563
(814) 893-5192

DAN CROKE
6117 Pioneer Jct Road
Duluth, MN 55804
(218) 525-2411

J & K FUR EXCHANGE
Ralph Degesie
2893 S-M65
Whittemore, MI 48770
(517) 756-2473

A nice stack of red fox!

Buckshot with a fleshing beam.

7 Tanning Fur

anning furs is a lot of hard work but if you invest the effort, your fur will last many years. There are several methods for tanning fur—emergency tanning, home tanning with homemade solutions, home tanning with commercial products and commercial tanning. While each of these will be discussed, it is worth mentioning here that you will get the best results from a commercial tanner. The tanning factory has the best equipment and the human resources necessary to do the hard work involved.

The best commercial tanning facility I have ever used is Moyles Mink & Tanning out of Idaho. They mark your skin with your initials the day they receive it. Believe me, this is an important step; you want to make sure you get your fur back. I have sent furs out and received back furs that were clearly not the ones I brought them. I say "clearly" because I know the different colors in each of the furs I catch and the ones they presented to me had noticeably different colors. Therefore, if you are going to pay for the professional service why not go to the best company who offers the best prices and the quickest service? With some of the companies I have tried, I have waited up to nine months for my fur to come back. Moyles, on the other hand, guarantees you will have your fur back in 90 days. Enough said. You can reach them in the following ways: Moyles Mink and Tanning, 374 South 600 West, Heyburn, ID, 83336 or call (208) 678-3421.

If you prefer to tan your own pelts, you'll get your best results if you use a good commercial tanning solution. I carry Johnny Thorpe Indian Tan—the best home tanning solution I ever used.

The biggest mistake most people make is made before the tanning begins. It is very important that you flesh the animal—*remove all the fat and muscle off the skin.* The fat and grease react to the tanning solution and make it weaker. This affects the entire tanning process. So, the cleaner you make the pelt before you begin to tan, the better your results will be.

Emergency Tanning

Emergency tanning is done when you find yourself in a situation in the woods that requires immediate pelt tanning. For instance, if you are in immediate need of a pair of boots, a hat, gloves, or a coat or pants liner, here is what you do.

Skin the animal, flesh all the fat off and wash the pelt in a stream, making sure to remove all the dirt, mud, and burrs. Wring out and air dry. Then, build a good fire and place a large amount of green wood on top to get a smoking fire going. Place the pelt on a stick, tie it off with your boot strings so the pelt is stretched out on the fork of the stick. Place the skin over the smoke, about a foot or so above any flame. Slowly dry the pelt.

This is called smoke tanning and is a good emergency tan. It takes time and you have to be careful not to get the fur too close to the fire or to let it dry too quickly. After about an hour and half (for rabbit size animals) take the pelt off and stretch the skin. Check to see if the smoke has dried the pelt thoroughly. Place the skin in your hand and stretch one spot one way, then the other way. Look into the cracks. The pelt should look white.

Now you have to stretch the pelt every which way. Pull and stretch, for about an hour (again, for rabbit size animals). This makes the pelt pliable. Once that step is done, the pelt is ready to use for whatever you like. The larger and thicker the pelt, the longer this takes. A beaver would take about a half a day to complete. Make sure you don't dry the pelt too fast. You're *tanning* the pelt, not cooking it.

Another emergency tan is to use the method the Indians used— the primary ingredients being the animal's brain and bladder. Clean the pelt, just like before. Remove the bladder and pour it into a pot, mix the brains in. Bring to a boil. Remove the pot from the heat. Allow it to cool until you can put your hand in the pot without burning it. Then add the pelt. Make sure you use a stick to work the tanning solution into all the skin. You can add water to the mix at the beginning to make sure you have enough to cover the whole pelt. Leave the pelt in there for two days on thin skinned animals (such as rabbits) and up to four days for thick skinned animals (such as beavers).

Once you remove the pelt, rinse it in clean cool water. Then, work the pelt just like before. Stretching and pulling the whole time until the pelt is dry. This can take less than an hour for rabbits and up to four hours on beaver. This is pure hard work. If you get tired and want to quit, take water and moisten the pelt and roll it up. Then come back and start over.

Homemade Solution

One way to tan is by making up a homemade solution. You will use fresh, clean battery acid—1 oz. per one gallon of soft water or rainwater. *Remember, Safety, safety, safety first! Follow the same precautions as recommended by automobile repair manuals before handling battery acid—wear safety goggles, rubber gloves and a rubber apron.* Add the battery acid slowly into 4 gallons of water. Add your fresh pelt (not dried) that is fleshed with no fat or muscle on it.

Soak for two days for rabbit size pelts, up to four days for beaver and over a week for deer. Stir the pelt twice a day making sure none of it becomes dry. Check the pelt every few days the same way as described in smoke tanning. When the pelt is done, as you stretch it, the leather side of the cracked skin will be a white or cream color.

Rinse in three changes of water, wringing out the pelt each time. *Don't throw the tanning solution down the drain.* You have to neutralize it first with baking soda. Check and comply with all state and federal regulations on acid. If it is legal in your state or area, then pour it down the drain.

Now, work the pelt the same way as described for smoke tanning. Once it is soft and pliable, work in Neatsfoot Oil. You are now ready to make the pelt into useful articles like hats, mittens, coat linings, etc.

Another homemade recipe is oak tanning. This takes a long time, but here it is. Boil 1 gallon of acorns and oak leaves for 30 minutes in 5 gallons of clear water. Remove the leaves and acorns and, once cooled, add your pelts. Stir twice a day. After about two weeks, inspect the pelts to see how far the tanning solution has penetrated the hide. If more is needed, boil up a fresh batch and repeat. Smaller, thin hides will be done in 2–4 weeks. Large thick hides may take up to 3 months with six changes of the tanning solution.

After the pelt is removed, rinse and the break the hide as described before. There are more recipes out there if you are going to do this but, try doing the smaller, easier pelts first, then work your way up to your larger pelts.

Remember, *the better you flesh and the longer you work the pelt after it comes out of the solution, the better your finished pelt.* The stretching and pulling phase is the most important factor in getting you a nice, dried, soft, workable leather. Some people even use a log end to pull and work the pelt over. But this can only be done on a thick pelt, such as a beaver's. Like anything else, the first couple pelts you tan will be rough looking. Just keep at it. With each pelt, you will develop a system that works for you. It's just like riding a bike—at first it was hard but, the more you did it the easier it became.

Coyote (left) and gray fox (right)

Another option for your catches is taxidermy. Before you can mount the animals, you have to tan them. Mounted animals are an excellent source of trapping revenue and profit.

This bobcat was caught on a cold November day. While I was checking traps, I noticed that the set location was disturbed and the trap and drag were missing. I tracked him for a ¼ mile and when I found him, his death scream made the hair on the back of my neck stand straight up.

Eating Wild Game

have received many e-mails asking me about eating wild game. What kinds are edible? Is this or that particular animal better than another? My answer always revolves around "it depends on your situation at the time." In a true survival situation, all animals are edible. In WWII, many of the POW's lived on cooked rats. I have heard old trapping tales where the trapper had to kill and eat his dog sled team to survive. It all depends on what you call survival. The lobster at one time was considered a trashy shellfish, only good for fertilizer until someone cooked one up. It is all just a mindset. In a survival situation, you shouldn't mind and it won't matter.

I have eaten many different wild animals, including muskrats, beavers, raccoons, ground hogs, snapping turtles, frog legs, fresh water crawdads and more. And, I have found that, as with any type of food, it's all in the preparation and cooking.

People totally amaze me when it comes to cooking and preparing wild game. I talked with one deer hunter who refused to eat venison unless it was cooked well done. When I asked why, he said, "Because you have to kill all the parasites." What parasites? I have read about some cases of parasites, but come on, to say that every deer is not safe to eat is stretching it. This person came from the school of thought that contends that only domestically raised animals are safe to eat. If that were true, I would have been dead and buried 30 years ago.

Watch out for the rumor mill when it comes to wild game. Do any of these sound familiar?

You can't eat rabbits before the first frost.
Muskrats are only edible in months with an "R" in them.
Snapping turtles have to bleed for 24 hours.
Beavers are only good in the fall.
You have to age venison for at least five days before you can eat it.
Shotgun shot game must be eaten within 24 hours.
Porcupines are only safe to eat after the first snow.

My question to each person who believes those things is: Why????? Explain why this is true!!!!

Deer

After shooting and hanging the deer, the sooner you skin him the better. The skin peels off a fresh deer ten times easier than one that is cold. After skinning, I allow one day to age if the weather is below 40 degrees all day. Then I butcher the deer and eat some that night. If it is too warm, I butcher the deer right then and freeze for two days, then I eat him. I cook my venison in small bite size slices with onions, green peppers, and butter. Even the finicky love this method. Just cook on a medium heat—a pan full is done in 15 minutes. This is medium done and very tasty.

Grind the hamburger up and mix with beef hamburger because the venison needs fat to cook. (Deer fat is slim and tough and does not melt very well.) Or mix with ground sausage, which is especially good in chili.

Snapping Turtle

Snapping turtle takes a long time to cook. Here is one method an old timer told me. It takes about 12 hours, or until the meat is tender. If you cook and serve snappers too fast, make sure your fillings are in good shape because they are tough!

Place the meat in a cast iron pot and add 2 onions, 5 potatoes, 10 carrots, green pepper, a dash of allspice, salt and pepper. Add water to cover everything. Boil for 48 hours. Add water as need. After two full days of cooking, throw the soup away and eat the pot—it will taste better. Just kidding!

Freshwater Crawdads

Freshwater crawdads are just as tasty as shrimp. Cook them alive in boiling water for 10 minutes Remove and cool. Break off the tails and peel the shell, remove the blood vein. Dip in melted butter or bread and deep fry. Just like shrimp.

Muskrats

Muskrats get their name from the musk glands that are found under the skin on both sides of the anus. When cleaning the animal, make sure you remove them. If you are trapping, save them for making lure. In the fall, their glands are small, about the size of baked beans, and in the spring, they are quite large, about the size of a small banana pepper. They mark their territory and attract each other with them.

Remove the glands and thoroughly clean the animal. Soak in saltwater overnight, rinse and pat dry. Bake with bacon strips on it for 1 hour at 350°F. Or pan fry with a breading. Since baking makes the animal more tender, bake the older ones and pan fry the smaller ones.

Beavers

Beavers are the only animals whose taste depends on what it has been eating. If the beaver is eating pine bark, then you better be starving before you eat him. Pine bark makes for nasty tasting beaver. But, if they are eating good aspen, poplar, and cottonwood, they are very tasty. I have cooked them up in stews, and just like muskrats, the smaller ones are better pan-fried.

Cooking Tips For Wild Game

Experiment with spices, herbs and wild edibles in your cooking. Make up your own recipes with other ingredients your family likes.

To rid the meat of the wild game flavor, cover the wild game with 1 tablespoon of salt, inside and out, and then place in a crockpot; Cover with cold water. Let it set overnight.

I simmer most wild game on the stove for 4-5 hours. Let it cool, skim fat off the top, drain the water, take out the bones, then add fresh water and then make the recipe.

When using rabbit meat, treat it as chicken.

Most beef stew recipes can be used for wild game. Beaver, raccoon and muskrat are dark meats like beef. Pheasant, grouse, and quail are white meat, like chicken.

Wild Plant Seasonings

When eating wild plants, introduce them into your family's diets in small amounts. Wild plants have a lot of vitamins and minerals. If eaten in large doses, before your body adjusts to them, they can cause intestinal cramping and diarrhea. Garden grown vegetables don't even come close to the vitamin and mineral content of wild plants. Add a few, here and there, to soups and stews until your family becomes familiar with them.

When using wild plants, you must be sure to identify them EXACTLY. Ideally, find color photos. When you use wild plants, you are doing so at your own risk. I have presented those below to give you a feel for what is out there for you, but again, I recommend you get a comprehensive, illustrated book so you are certain you're finding and using the right plant. My selection: **The Official Pocket Edible Plant Survival Manual** by Robert W. Pelton. While it is black and white, it is a very handy reference—especially when you're actually in the woods. It fits right in your shirt pocket or backpack. It is available through QW, Inc (800)838-8854. *If you mention that you heard about it in this book you'll receive a "Buckshot reader" Discount!*

Coltsfoot–*(Tussilago farfara)*–Found along streams and in swamps. Flower appears before leaves.

To make salt, roll the leaves into small balls and place in the sun to dry. It takes about 4-5 days. Put them on a flat stone and burn them to ashes. The ashes are very saline and make a wonderful salt substitute. The taste is very surprising.

Spice Bush–Allspice*(Linders benzoin)*–This grows in damp woods and along streams. Dry the red berries in the sun and then crush into a powder. Use in place of allspice.

Vinegar–Get sap from sugar maple trees and birch trees. Let the sap ferment in the sun, then strain through a cloth. Flies will be attracted to this, but that's okay, they will aid in the fermentation process.

Sweet Bay–*(Magnolia virginiana)*–A small tree known to most as swamp magnolia or swamp laurel.

The Red Bay–*(Persea borbonia)*–Also a small tree with red bark; the leaves look similar to evergreen leaves.

Dry both of the Bay leaves in the sun until they crumble when you pick them up. Great flavor for stuffing, stews, and soups.

Violet–*(violet odorata)*–Only use the common variety. It is the only edible kind. It adds a very delicious flavor to anything. Wild okra is a cousin to this plant. Only use the flowers and leaves. Add a little dried violet to your flour for a very tasty bread or biscuits.

Wild Mustard–*(Brassica nigra)*–Dry the seeds and then pound them into a powder. Use as you would use store bought powdered mustard.

Recipes For Wild Game

Cooking wild game is just like cooking any type of meat—you have to know how so that it comes out right. Once you start trapping, you will soon start collecting different animals. After removing the pelt, the first thing you do, just like any game animal, is gut it. *Never gut a fur bearer before skinning if you are selling the pelt.* This is the main difference between hunting and trapping.

Gutting the animal

You gut all animals the same way. Carefully place your knife under the stomach membrane and cut up to the rib-cage. Set the knife down and pull open the membrane—use your thumb and poke throw the membrane separating the stomach and intestines from the heart and lungs. Reach up and grab the windpipe and pull all the guts out.

You then have to carefully cut out the bladder. The bladder is a light color sack full of fluid (urine). *You do not want to puncture this as it can contaminate the meat.* Grab the bladder and twist it tight, then, using a sharp knife, cut the bottom tube and pull the bladder out. If you rip or puncture the bladder, immediately wash out the area the urine spilled on.

Next, you have to cut out the anus. Using a sharp knife, cut around it on the outside; on a small animal, reach in from the inside, grab the intestine tube and pull it out. On medium and large animals you may have to use your knife in different spots to get the tubes to release. Look over the inside and pull out any remains. Cut the head off and remove the windpipe.

Wash the animal thoroughly. If you plan to cook it soon, cut the animal up into pieces and soak in salt water over night. Place in the refrigerator. Soaking over night removes any blood and helps to tenderize the meat a little.

I have given you just a few recipes to get you started. You'll soon be able to tell that I am not a chef, but I do know and like good tasting food! Since everyone has different tastes, start with these and modify them along the way to cater to your family's preferences. (All temperatures are in Farenheit.)

Rabbit or Marsh Rabbit Sauce and Noodles.

I like simple easy recipes. This is one of my favorite ways to cook rabbit or marsh rabbits (muskrats).

Par boil the pieces for an hour. Remove from heat and let cool. Cut off all the meat and toss the bones away. Place the meat in an oven dish, cover with 1 can of cream of mushroom soup and one can of water. Season with salt and pepper. Bake for 1 hour at 350°. Cook the noodles so they are done when the meat has finished baking.

Wash and drain the noodles and add to the oven dish. Stir them in. Add water if needed. Bake for 30 minutes. Serve. This is outstanding and an easy to do recipe. If you are working and want it really tender, place in a slow cooker at low and go to work. When you come home, cook the noodles and bake for 20 minutes.

Barbecue Raccoon Delight

The wife of a friend showed me this and I never turn down a chance to eat her barbecue raccoon. To tell the truth it was hard to tell the difference between the coon and beef. The secret is to trim off as much fat as you can.

Bake on a rack at 350° with a pan to catch the drippings. The size and fat content will determine the length of time you bake. A small, trim raccoon, with hardly any fat, should be done in an hour. Then, cover with your favorite barbecue sauce and cook for another 30 minutes.

Beaver soup

Remember what I said about beaver—if they are eating pine, cedar, or fir trees you better be starving if you are going to cook them. But if they are eating poplar, cottonwoods, or other soft leave trees, the beaver is excellent to eat. I have barbecued them just like raccoons and they taste like beef. In the colder months, after running traps or deer hunting all day, I want soup or stew to warm me up when

I get home. My wife has a deer stew recipe that is so great she should patent it. Maybe I can get her to write it out.

I like the 20 to 40 pound beaver for this one. Par-boil the meat until it is tender enough to peel off the bones with a fork. This may take an hour or two. Toss the bones and add potatoes, onions, carrots, green beans or peas, salt, pepper, and onion salt. Cook all day. I like thick soup so I add a package of beef gravy to it. This is a great way to warm up after a long day in the bush.

Northern White Beans and Beaver

A friend of mine showed me this recipe. He par-boiled the beaver and ripped off the meat. Then at midnight added the northern white beans and meat in the slow cooker. This was at a low setting and cooked well into the next day. At 6 PM we had one of the best beaver meals I have ever tasted. Talk about filling, this is a great deer camp recipe.

My Favorite Squirrel Recipe

My wonderful wife cooks squirrel this way. First sauté the squirrel in butter or margarine. Place in a baking pan and add cornbread stuffing, onions, salt and pepper. Cover everything with brown gravy and bake, covered, at 350° for 1 hour. This is the best squirrel I have ever had.

My Favorite Venison Recipe

Cut the steak up into 2 inch strips about ½ inch thick. Brown onions and green pepper. Add the steak and cook at medium heat turning as needed for about 15 minutes. Serve hot. I have not met one person who does not love this.

Ruffed Grouse Breast

A friend of mine used to shoot and give me all his grouse. One day, I convinced him to cook one up. He filleted the breast out and his wife cooked them up like skinless chicken breasts. I never got another grouse from him. He started hunting them big time and his wife was after him to get more. I should have kept my mouth shut. Just try it and you will be surprised.

Take one grouse per person. Fillet the breast off the bird. Cook in butter with salt and pepper for 15 minutes at a medium heat. This is better than chicken could ever taste.

Fried Muskrat
1 muskrat
½ cup milk
1 teaspoon salt and 1 tablespoon salt
1 quart water
½ cup breadcrumbs
1 egg yolk (or dried eggs)
4 tablespoons fat

Wash and clean the muskrat. Rub the 1 tablespoon salt on meat, inside and out, place in a crock with 1 quart of cold water. Let it set overnight. Mix the egg and milk in a small bowl, set aside. Put the muskrat in a stockpot, cover with cold water and bring to a boil over high heat, then simmer for 30 minutes.

Remove from heat and let it get to room temperature. Remove muskrat and cut into 2 inch squares. Dip the pieces into the milk and egg bowl, sprinkle with the tsp. of salt and the breadcrumbs. Melt fat in frying pan, lower the heat and fry the pieces, browning on all sides. Simmer for 2 hours, or until meat is tender.

"The muskrat has been given a bad rap by having the word 'rat' associated with it. A more appropriate name would have been marsh rabbit."

Raccoon and Beans

>   2 raccoon legs
>   1 bag of beans (any variety)
>   2 whole onions, or 3 tablespoons dried onion
>   3 strips of bacon, or 2 teaspoons of bacon substitute
>   1 tablespoon of dried peppers
>   Salt and pepper

Soak beans over night. Bake raccoon legs at 350° for 2 hours. Add beans to a slow cooker or to a stockpot and cook on low heat. Fry bacon strips until crisp. Add all other ingredients. Cook for 10 hours on very low heat. Take bones out and serve. You can make up 2 cups of gravy to add as flavor and for a thickener.

Beaver and Dandelion Soup

>   4 tablespoons fat
>   2 lbs. of chopped beaver
>   2 wild onions, finely chopped
>   1 cup arrowhead tubers, finely chopped
>   2 cups young dandelion leaves, or ¼ cup dried
>   ½ teaspoon of salt and pepper

Melt fat in a saucepan. When fat is sizzling hot, add the chopped onions, sauté until a clear color, not brown. Add arrowhead tubers and dandelion leaves. Stir for 5 minutes. Add the soup stock, salt and pepper. Bring to a boil, simmer 15 minutes. Serve over freshly baked bannock. (See Recipe below.)

Fresh dandelion can have a very bitter taste so if you're going to use it, boil the leaves for 5 minutes, drain, add fresh water, boil again for 5 minutes, drain, then add them to your recipe.

Bannock

I don't like carrying bread when I'm in the bush because it is always getting smashed to pieces. So, I read about how the old trappers who scouted for weeks at a time made their own bread. The recipe is quite simple. All you need is general flour, baking powder, salt and butter, or some type of oil for the pan.

You build your fire and, as it is burning down to coals, you mix ¾ cup of flour, one tablespoon of baking powder, a little salt and mix dry. Slowly add water and mix into a stiff dough. Don't add too much water. You want it like bread dough, not pancake mix thin.

I have an enamel 7 inch frying pan that is perfect for this. Place the pan on the coals of the fire to heat up. Add butter until it is melted and the pan is lightly coated. Add your dough and spread it out into the size of pita loaf. Cook one side, over a medium heat away from the flame, until you can flip it over without breaking it in half. Once flipped, add some more butter and cook. The bread will raise about ½ to ¾ its wet size. Check with a sliver of wood until no dough sticks to it.

This is really awesome—it's like having fresh baked bread every time. We made peanut butter and jam sandwiches by cutting the loaf in half. Try it with summer sausage, baked beans, and eggs, and of course, Beaver and Dandelion soup.

Beaver Soup Stock

3 pounds beaver, bones and meat
1 cup arrowhead tubers
1 cut up wild onion
½ cup fat (bacon preferred)
1 tablespoon salt
¼ cup shredded mint leaves
3 quarts cold water
3 cups cattail shoots
2 tablespoons allspice
2 bay leaves

Boil meat and bones in 4 quarts of water, then cool. Skim fat off the top. Take the meat out of the pot and discard the water and bones. Melt fat in a frying pan. Brown meat on all sides. Put back into stockpot and add 3 quarts of water and all other ingredients. Cover and bring to a boil, then simmer for 4-6 hours. Put in a cool place and skim off any fat on top. You can add any vegetables you like, dried or fresh.

Beaver Tail Soup

Bones from a beaver
4 bay leaves
1 beaver tail
1 tablespoon of allspice
4 quarts water
1 teaspoon of salt
3 teaspoons of dried dandelion
½ teaspoon dried violet
4 wild onions
1 teaspoon wild mustard

Separate the bones from the meat, break the bones into 6 inch pieces. Cut the tail meat into 6 inch strips. Put all of this into a stockpot with 4 quarts of water, 1 teaspoon of salt, 1 onion. Bring to a boil and simmer for 2 hours.

Take off the stove and set it some place cool, for about 2-3 hours. Let all the fat rise to the top of the pot. Skim fat off. Take the bones out of the pot. Return to the stove and add all the other ingredients, add more water as needed. Cook for one hour. Serve. Add any other dried vegetables you have that you like. Take the beaver tail and put it over an open flame, burn the scaly skin. Cool, peel off burnt skin and eat the delicious white meat underneath.

Creamed Wild Onions

20 small wild onions
¼ teaspoon of pepper
4 tablespoons of flour
1 teaspoon dried peppers
2 cups of milk
4 tablespoons of fat
1 teaspoon of salt
¼ teaspoon dried chickweed

Melt fat in frying pan. Add flour, stirring when the mixture forms small balls. Add the milk slowly. Add all ingredients, except onions. In another saucepan, cover onions with water and bring to a boil. Boil about 15 minutes or until onions are tender.

Remove from heat, drain, add to white sauce. Serve. This is a great base for any creamed soup. If making soup, double the recipe and add potatoes and other dried vegetables. You can add any meat you have handy. If adding meat, cook meat separately for two hours, then add.

Venison Stew

2 pounds of venison and bones
6 potatoes and any vegetables you have (dried or fresh)
2 cups gravy
4 onions or 2 tablespoons dried onions
4 whole allspice
Salt and pepper

Cook the meat, as stated in tips. Add all ingredients in the stockpot, simmer for 4-5 hours. About 1 hour before serving, make up the 2 cups of gravy and add to stew. Very tasty.

Squirrel Surprise

    2-3 squirrels
    Make up one quart of stuffing
    Make up 2 cups of gravy

Fry squirrel on low heat, browning on all sides. Set aside. Make up the stuffing mixture from whatever you have one hand. Put it in a dutch oven, lay the squirrel on top of the stuffing, pour gravy over it all. Bake at 350° for 1 hour. Serve.

Rabbit Stew With Dumplings

    1 rabbit
    1 large dandelion root
    ¾ cup flour
    2 teaspoons coltsfoot salt
    Cold water
    2 tablespoons of baking powder
    ½ teaspoon salt
    2 mint leaves (Dried)
    1 egg (or powered egg)
    15-20 arrowhead tubers
    ½ cup milk
    3 wild onions

Cut the skinned rabbit into serving pieces. Place in a stockpot, add water to cover. Bring to a boil and simmer for 1 hour. Take the rabbit out of the stockpot and separate the meat from the bones. Return the rabbit meat to the stockpot. Add everything but the flour, baking powder, salt, egg and milk. Bring to a boil, then simmer for 2 hours.

Mix the ¾ cup flour, 2 tablespoons baking powder, ½ teaspoon salt, 1 egg and milk. Add dry ingredients first, then the egg, then slowly mix in the milk. Drop the dumpling mixture by the spoonful into the rabbit stew. Cook for 15–20 minutes. Serve.

Beverages From The Wild

Dandelion Coffee

Use the roots. Wash and scrape them well. Dry them on a low heat in the oven, or wrap them in foil and put them on the embers. The roots will turn black. Cut into small pieces and grind. You can mix with your regular coffee or it can be used in place of coffee.

Sunflower Coffee

The Seneca Indians used to make this. Roast the sunflower seeds. Then pound them, separate the shells from the seeds. Pour water over the seeds.

New Jersey Tea (*Ceanothus americanus*)

This was used during the Revolutionary War as a substitute for tea. Use the leaves. Dry them and steep.

Cherry or Birch Bark Tea

Use the bark and young twigs from the trees. Steep young twigs and bark for 15–20 minutes. Tastes similar to wintergreen tea.

Bear Berry or Service Berry Cider

Pick the berries and scald them, until soft. Then crush and make into a pulp. Add as much water as pulp. Strain through a cloth. Cool, has a spicy, acid taste.

Strawberry Leaf Tea

Pick the young strawberry leaves and dry them. Steep as for tea. Steep for about 30 minutes, these leaves take a little longer. This tea can be used for colds and sore throats, not to mention that it has a very pleasant taste. Try adding a little dried violet to it. Very good to drink.

As you can see, these recipes are part of my family's regular diet. Eating wild game and living off the land are not only for survival situations. In fact, a very important rule to self-sufficient living is to adjust to the lifestyle before you find yourself in a survival or emergency situation. You don't want to be learning new cooking methods or eating habits when you're on the brink of starvation.

At any rate, if circumstances place you and your family in such a situation, I am convinced that trapping skills will always put more meat on the table than hunting skills, except in the states where elk and moose are plentiful. But, then again, I'm convinced that in those states, in a survival situation, the elk and moose herds will not last very long.

Therefore, the individual who is consistently spending time trapping in the woods will realize and come to admit that *living* fully off the land becomes the same as surviving off the land. And, over time, his or her family will barely recognize the difference.

Trapping Summer Pests and Nuisance Animals

Every summer, people who need my assistance with problem animals contact me. This can be very beneficial to me in two ways. The first, of course, is the extra cash; the going rate is $40.00 per animal. The second advantage is that I am usually able to pick up the owner's permission for fall trapping.

Sometimes this works really well and other times it is not worth the trouble. One time I was called about problem beavers tearing up a pond. I arrived and asked the landowner if anyone else had tried to trap the beaver. He said no. So I set two #330 Conibears thinking that I'd have the job finished in two days and, in exchange, I would walk away with permission to trap a 300 acre farm. Two days later, I still hadn't trapped a beaver. The beavers were trap shy. I approached the landowner and asked why the beavers were acting so strange. He told me he had tried for a month to shoot the beaver with .22's and shotguns.

I walked the whole pond until I found the bank dens. I removed my normal sets and placed them in the entrance to the bank dens. The next day, I had both beavers and the job was finished. That fall, I set up for trapping fox and after three days the farmer asked me to remove the traps because his wife was worried their dog would get caught. So I pulled the traps. The next spring when new beavers moved in I charged $25 a beaver. This was a fair price considering my time, equipment cost, and transportation costs. So, when I know I am providing a needed service, I charge for it. I suggest you do the same.

Few people question paying for this service; especially after they run down to the local hardware store and find out a #330 Conibear costs $27.99 plus $12.95 for the setting tool. At that point, they know it is well worth their money to hire me. Besides, the guy who buys the trap and sets it for beaver usually misses. Then, the beaver becomes trap shy and if the guy doesn't tell you he's attempted and failed to catch the animal, you can waste a lot of time. I charge $45 per animal on trap shy ones because of all the extra work involved. Most people are really good about it and gladly pay just to get rid of the problem animals.

We have vacation cottages in the area where we live. Recently, I worked two cases—red squirrels and ground hog. The ground hog was interesting because of the location of the den. I only brought one #220 Conibear with me thinking I would set the den hole and be done. Well, the den was under the front porch and the little critter had dug two holes under the foundation with about four inches of clearance, too small for a #220. The landowner said the ground hog entered on the side of the front porch. I found the trail and set it, blocking it off with sticks. This left the other hole open. I thought "no problem—he will leave one hole and enter the other and it will be all over."

I went back the next day. No ground hog! "OK," I figured, "I need another trap." But, the guy was having a garage sale and I didn't want to set the second trap in the middle of it. Day three: still no ground hog. "That's it!" I thought. I brought another #220 Conibear trap and crawled under the porch. Using a garden trowel, I dug a path down deep enough for the #220 to fit under the porch. I set the trap and stabilized it by pushing it against the 2 x 6 frame and the ground. It took a few minutes to work the trap in and make sure it was dug out enough on both sides.(It's important to make sure both sides are clear so the trap can fire and close all the way.) Then I placed firewood on both sides of the traps from the den hole all the way out to the front of the porch. I blocked off the other set the same way. "No more playing around." Whether that ground hog was going in or coming out, he was mine! I left thinking "one more check and this job is over."

The next day the ground hog was flattened in the #220. Which set do you think took the animal? The one under the porch. I followed his tracks in the dirt path right to the #220 Conibear. The trap hit him perfectly, just behind the neck and I think he died instantly because the trap was in the same spot where I set it. The landowner was happy because the ground hog was doing some serious damage to the structural integrity of the foundation, so much so that he had to patch the foundation.

The next job was for red squirrels. Red squirrels are the smallest of squirrels and, once they've entered a vacation cottage, they can do hundreds of dollars worth of damage in a few weeks. These particular red squirrels thought the cottage was built for them and had really torn up the place. I took some #110 Conibears, a few nails and peanut butter to solve the problem.

The cottage had a little attic space, which was where the squirrels had entered the cabin. I climbed up there and pounded two nails per trap in the rafter boards. The nails were spaced so the #110 was set over them and squeezed tight so the trap was firmly held. The nails, on the outside of the trap, stabilized the trap and kept the squirrels from knocking over the trap. I baited the trigger with a piece of bread smeared in peanut butter. I set three traps and left. The next day there were two dead squirrels. I re-set the two traps and left them for one more day.

The last day on the job I took one more red squirrel and the problem was solved. I showed the land owner where the squirrels were getting in so he could patch the hole to prevent any more from thinking they had found a new home.

Bats are currently bringing in respectable money (up to $100 an hour). This is because they frequently invade attics in homes and are considered the most feared animal in North America. Thus, people are willing to pay good money to have them removed, but catching them is not for everybody. First, bat droppings are categorized as hazardous waste so you must be licensed in most states before you can even begin. Second, you must be willing and able to climb into attics and work on ladders two to three stories high.

I just started trapping bats and the process is fairly straight forward. Basically, you must discover how the bats are entering the house and close it off with a device called an exclusion tube. The exclusion tube allows the bats to fly out but not reenter. There are also traps specifically for bats available on the market. Most of them are the live cage types so the bat can be released outside after being caught.

In Florida, alligator removal is also bringing top dollar. In 1998, 12,865 permits were issued to remove problem alligators. Once on the endangered species list, alligators have been reduced to a threatened species (although there are over 1 million of them in the state) which allows the state to issue permits for removal in order to protect adults, children and dogs. You must become a state licensed trapper before a permit will be issued to you. This is not a job for the amateur and I do not recommend getting into this.

As you can see, I encourage you to pursue the same types of summer jobs that I do—those that are short, safe and solved with Conibears. I use the #110 for squirrels, and the #220 for ground hogs, raccoons, and skunks, and the #330 for beaver.

The only time I have to use leg-holds for these animals is to solve trap-shy animal problems. This is one way you can pick up extra cash and gain permission for the Fall trapping. You can quickly pay for the cost of your traps and then in the Fall, all your equipment will be paid for and your furs will be pure profit. Check your local game laws and make sure you don't need any special license to do this. *Tell the landowner you are not responsible if his or her pets get caught—make an agreement before you set traps.* Check with the local neighbors and let them know that traps are set in the area and that they need to protect their animals from wandering on other people's property. As always, neither the publisher nor this author takes responsibility for your actions or risk. So again, be responsible.

Just a word of caution—some people are strange about trapping. Don't get in a yelling match with a do-gooder! If in doubt, don't set a trap without making sure a dog can't get caught. One way to trap ground hogs in fields where dogs may run is to place plywood pieces over the den holes leaving just a little opening. The ground hogs will quickly dig out a hole large enough to fit under. Then all you have to do is lift the board, set the traps, stabilize, stake and wire off. Place the board back over the hole. This should keep dogs out.

One nice thing about summer trapping is that it is good practice for the fall. You will make some mistakes but you will learn. Once fall rolls around, you will be a better trapper and you will be able to catch more animals. In addition, you should have some farms to trap. Create a sign calling yourself the local rodent remover, or problem animal solver, or whatever. Post it at your local feed store and soon you will be in business. It is a lot of fun, so why not give it a try?

 *Questions and Answers*

he following Questions and Answers have been taken from my web-site, www.survival-center.com/buckshot. I have been fielding these questions and posting the latest trapping news for over a year. In the process, I have certainly learned as much as the people who have been asking me the questions. Please feel free to contact me. I'd like to hear your questions and I'd certainly be interested in hearing any comments you're willing to share about this book, especially your success stories!

When you're out for extended periods of time, what do you do for your drinking water?

I have tried everything. I once bought a water filter from a popular surplus place and it was junk. It took two hands and five minutes of squeezing like I was Arnold to get one cup of water. But then, I found the perfect solution: The Pres2Pur water filter. It comes with a special canteen that you fill with river water. Screw in the filter and (easily!) squeeze your water out. It's incredible how good it works. It lasts for up to 200 gallons of water. The best part about this it that it frees you up from carrying the added weight of water. Plus, when the canteen becomes warm from the summer heat, you can dump the water out, find a cool clean spot in the river and refill. There's nothing like having fresh, clean, cool water during the heat of the day. They retail for around $30.00 and can be ordered by calling: 888-842-6542 or visiting www.safewateranywhere.com.

How do you make waxed dirt?

Waxed dirt is simple to make yourself and is used for freeze-proofing. Take shredded wax and melt it in over sifted, dry dirt. You can do this on hot summer days with a black piece of plastic, which will absorb the sunlight. Make sure you mix the dirt and wax together so all is covered with wax. After it is all mixed in, store in clean 5 gal. buckets with a snap on lid. Another way is to melt the wax in the oven at 200°. Be careful, wax is flammable.

What are the different types of freeze-proofing?

Waxed dirt is one of the best. Spray anti-freeze, propylene glycol will work, over the dirt, covering your trap. Use ½ oz to 1 oz of sprayed anti-freeze per set. Cattail duff can also be used for freeze-proofing around marshes or lakes. Just make sure you place it on the bottom, too. Two pieces of wax paper crumpled up and re-opened also works well. Place one piece on top of the trap and one on the bottom. Cover with a light coating of sifted snow.

Can you catch fleas from the animals that are infected, when you are skinning them?

Sure—the fleas will jump on and stay on you. Get a plastic bag and spray it with Raid. Then toss the animals in it when you get to the truck.

I went coon hunting the other night and took my 4-year-old walker female. She treed a nice 30 pounder first, and while I was skinning it she went on to tree another one. I had to hurry up and skin the first one and never even looked at the fur. When I got to her, she had one bigger than the first one. Anyway, when I got back to the truck, I noticed that the first one had two bare spots on its back about 1 inch wide and about 6 or 7 inches long. It kind of grossed me out because I had already skin it out. Was this mange, or some other disease?

Get to your doctor quickly. Mange is a parasite that eats the skin below the hair line causing the hair to fall out. You can't see them with the naked eye but you will be itching like mad. Did your dog tear into the coon? You may have to take him to the vet also. Were you wearing gloves? Make sure you wash all clothing the skin touched.

One of my reds at a certain farm had mange. The next one didn't appear to have it. How many foxes do you have to take from a small area to significantly reduce the spread of this disease? Thanks. (This question was asked in the fall.)

Foxes are now on what is called the fall shuffles. So it could have just come into the farm from another county. Make sure you bury the diseased one so the disease doesn't spread. You could trap them all out and more will come.

I just had a red fox pull out from the trap as I approached the set—what a bummer. How much grief will this fox cause me with digging, etc.? How hard will it be to catch this guy? I'll know him if I get him. Suggestions on tactics appreciated.

If you can't snare him, then you will have to trail set him with no lure or bait. Good luck.

I have been at it for about three weeks and things have definitely slowed. Fox signs are there, but they're ignoring the sets that previously connected. I'm using mostly dirt-holes, with a territorial lure. Should I make brand new flat sets with different lure in

same area (it's sod, so it's hard to camouflage) or try the same farm in a different location or...? Advice greatly appreciated.

Three weeks on the same farm? Move to a new farm. If you want the last few fox, you have to make all new sets and change your lure and bait. The fox are bored with your bait and scent after three weeks.

A single red fox kept today from being a total disaster. Most of my traps were sprung; some were pulled to the end of the chain, others were just sitting on the ground in the beds. I'm usually very careful about being clean, though I tried waxing for the first time. I re-set the sprung traps. Advise, please. Thank you.

Are you sure that you are getting a rock solid trap bed? Also, make sure that your trap positioning is correct. If the fox feels the trap wiggle under his foot, then he will dig it up. Once he figures it out, he goes to other sets just for the fun of it. Another reason for your problem may be because you are using the same lure that someone else is using. So, re-set and go to a new area. Leave him for seed.

How long should you leave fur (coons & fox) on the stretcher?

Fox, coyote, bobcat, and fisher—one day skin side out, 2-3 days fur side out. Coons—sometimes 5 to 7 days, if you fleshed them perfectly—3–4 days.

I heard of one farm where a guy trapped 28 red fox in 30 days. How do you pick out one of those 28 fox farms?

I have a couple of those primary areas on my trap line. When the fox pups shuffle, they primarily follow waterways and other long running barriers and these particular farms will normally have two or more long running barriers that come together and create a funnel area.

I am a novice trapper in his first year and would like some advice as to ascertaining the sex of a beaver. I have caught 10 so far and I am curious how you can tell the difference. I understand that both sexes have the same exposed genitalia. I would really like an informed answer to this seemingly stupid question?

The beaver plumbing is indoors, so the best way to find out is to open the beaver up. Make a cut from the anal area up the belly about six or eight inches. Using a knife, cut the hide away from this area on each side of the slit. You should notice the castors—they are normally the largest pair of anything in this area and can be cream color to dark gray. If you feel these castors, they feel mushy and sometimes you can feel lumps in them. The elongated red or pink tubular looking things are the oil glands. If you look at where the castors come together and see a whitish tube, about the diameter of a pencil, this is the penis—hence a male. If there is no whitish tube there—it's a female. I can usually take my index finger and thumb and squeeze the area above the anal area and be able to tell if there is a penis or not, without having to open them up—but I have been fooled. The only way to be sure is to open them up for a peek.

I need to know how to trap beavers that have dammed up a ditch. I have some #220 Conibear traps, but I do not know how to set them up for beaver. Can anybody tell me an easy way to trap these things? I live in Illinois.

#220 is a questionable beaver trap, you may be able to trap them with it if you can find a small ramp coming out of the ditch to a tree that is cut into the bank. Do you have any snares? Snare them where they are climbing out of the water toward good feed on the trees. Good luck, boy. If you spook them with that #220, they will be really hard to trap. Can you get a #330 or a #3 leg-hold?

What is the best foothold for beavers? Would a #3 offset Bridger be sufficient in a drowning set? What about lures for this set? Any help would be appreciated I've never trapped beaver before and I think I might like to try it. Thanks.

There is a lot to this question, and I'll try to be as informative, yet brief, as possible. First off, if I were to use a #3 coil it would be a Bridger or Northwoods. However, I'd four coil it and it wouldn't be offset. There have been too many times that I've held beavers by one or two toes from the back foot. I'm afraid that an offset would have allowed the toes to slip out.

155

You need a powerful trap to hold a beaver by the back foot below the ankle because the back foot is tapered and has no pads to prevent the trap from slipping off. A beaver can and does pull out of traps when caught by the back foot below the ankle. It's surprising how easily the foot will come out of a trap. There are many sets that can be used with a foothold. There is the castor mound set with lure. This set usually will get a back foot. There is the food set with lure. This can get a front foot when positioned correctly.

There is the crossover set. This is where the trap is positioned usually at the top or bottom of the trail that the beavers use to go over the dam. This will either get a front or back foot. I like using lure at this set because the beaver may not have intended to go over the dam when swimming by. The lure will get the beaver actively looking for the lure source and increase the chance that he will go over the crossover. There are many more sets for the foothold, but these are the ones I use the most. Dam crossover sets will catch more critters than just beavers. It can catch any critter going over the dam including otters, muskrats, turtles, nutria and anything else that will take that path. Also, care must be taken on setting the trap at the top of the dam. Many land animals use a beaver dam as a bridge to cross the stream. These include deer, fox, dogs, bobcats, coon, coyotes, humans, etc. I usually put up a stick near the trap to cause any animals traversing the dam to go around where the trap is set. Hope this helps.

How careful do you have to be with human scent, disturbance around the set, etc. for trapping mink? Thanks.

Go trap a pile of muskrats—they're the best mink bait out there. More paper has been wasted on how smart minks are than any other animal except foxes. If the trap is under water, scent doesn't matter because the water is covering the trap. On dry land, wear gloves and adjust your traps so they have light pan tension. You will catch them. Just don't leave any footprints next to the set.

I plan on doing some marten trapping this fall and need to know some quick and easy ways to trap marten. Also, what is the best way to determine where marten travel?

Use a box set with a #120 Conibear. Place your bait at the back of the box and nail it to a tree. Check your area's regulations to make sure that it is legal. Use a piece of fish, beaver or squirrel with a good lure, the fresher the bait the better. Marten prefer heavily timbered country where the growth is mainly spruce, balsam, and hemlock that's close to the timberline. Nothing comes quick and easy.

A few days ago, I added a weasel set to a hollow log. This morning, the area was disturbed (although not too much) but the #1 long-spring had one of its jaws pulled out and one of the surrounding saplings looked like a miniature chainsaw had gone on a rampage. I'm no expert on weasel dentures, but some of the marks seemed awfully tiny for a coon. Can a weasel pull the jaws out of the frame? Incidentally, I saw a weasel hunting the same area last deer season. Any thoughts on this? The ground was frozen, so no tracks. No blood, either. I could have been robbed, but I don't know.

If that was a weasel, you better move. (Grin) My guess it was a coon or a huge mink or a fisher. That would be my best guess. I doubt seriously that a weasel can ever pull the jaws out. What was the bait and how close is it to water? I had an otter do that to a muskrat set once.

Chicken skins as bait. It's a long way to water, in a heavily forested area. That's what I thought about a weasel pulling the jaws out. Very few fishers have been known to be on that mountain, but probably it was a coon. I just didn't expect one there. Interesting.

157

What do you think of the 110 magnums? Do they last longer and are they worth the extra money?

All the magnum traps come from a design that was being made to kill the animal quicker. My personal opinion is that I don't like the jaw design, they are hard to stabilize and if you slip, they close hard. (Ouch) I like beaver or muskrat to fight the trap and get into deep water so they don't spook the other animals. The tests I have read give a little quicker kill time on the animals. For me, I will stay with standard Conibears and save the money.

How do you use sawdust to help flesh a coon?

I've heard you can do this with an old clothes dryer that turns, but has a broken heating element. Throw in the fleshed coon hide and some sawdust and run the dryer. In 15 minutes you are supposed to have a clean pelt. You have to wash it. The sawdust absorbs the fats, so some people layer it on thick instead of just sprinkling it on. Let it sit for 30 minutes and wash it out. I just flesh more, it takes less time.

I have trapped a stretch of a small river for a few years. Someone has moved in and beat me to the coons. Does anyone know how long will it be before coons move into the area again? It was full of coon sign before the season but is almost void of sign now.

Are you sure someone beat you? Coons are funny critters. If some cornfield just got harvested, the coons will quit the water and head for the field or a wild apple orchard because grapes or acorns suddenly taste better than fish. They will be where the food is, especially when a cold snap comes. They will always head for where they think has the most food. Set up some on the creek but look around for some other food source. Good luck.

How do you get close enough to a skunk to inject them without getting sprayed? I'll bet I caught a dozen of the dang things last year, just shot each of them with a .22. Every one of them sprayed before dying.

Switch to .22 short hollow points and shoot them in the lungs. They won't spray 90% of the time. Use acetone on a long pole. Come in slowly and then inject them.

Someone help me out again! Tell me once again, how does weather affect coons', minks' and otters' animal movement? If there is no real weather change, how long do you leave your traps? Thanks, Forgetful!

Coon move in five to seven days; a month is not too long to wait for otter and mink. Weather (cold) makes the predator eat more so they cover more ground looking for food.

I am trapping a real nice rat pond and I have seen some mink tracks. My problem is that there is no bank, it's all flat around the pond. I would set dirt holes but the ground is too wet and the trap would freeze over night. Can anyone help me figure out a way to catch some mink here?

If you have any kind of a bank, even four inches tall on land, dig a deep hole 14-18 inches deep, straight in the bank, just wide enough to place a #110 Conibear over the hole.

Shove a skinned Muskrat in the back of the hole. Place the #110 over the hole with two small sticks on the bottom jaws to keep the trap off the ground and from freezing. Stake the trap. I have heard of people catching coons in sets like this. You might want to set a #1½ coil spring on a drowner so you can take both coon and mink.

Hey all you expert trappers out there, I'm wanting to make some home made canine bait out of deer and beaver meat. What do I have to do to taint it to the right stage and then how is the sodium B. used? Do you first mix the S.B. with water and then add the meat to it or what? Don't be bashful, give me some advice. After all if I'm crazy enough to ask these questions for the whole world to see, I at least deserve some help.

That is a good question with a thousand answers. Here is one way. Chunk the meat up into roughly 1 inch squares. Fill a bucket

159

with it. When the wife says you either throw it out or she is leaving, add the sodium benzoate. Depending on the temperature outside, taint it for about a week, then add the sodium benzoate.

I've heard it said by one of the best canine men in the country that a speed-dipped trap is not a clean trap. They say that it's supposed to be OK for water sets and for coon and bobcats, but it will cause up to 30% losses on the fox and coyotes. Is this true? I've stuck to dying and waxing even though it involves a lot more work.

30% losses on speed dip is about right. Sure, you will catch fox and coyote, but you're missing 3 for every 7 you take home. I stick with the old logwood dye and wax for all my fox and coyote sets. Of course, it's your choice. This is just what I have found out.

Buckshot, I know you have trapped and called all animals, but do you have possum calls and directions for using them in stock? Please advise. Also, what's a good set for trap shy possums? I can't seem to catch them, foxes and coons keep getting in my traps. Any help appreciated.

The best possum call in the world is a perfect dirt hole made for fox. I swear to God! Make the perfect dirt hole set just for fox and for a 1000 miles, every possum will come a running. There will be fist fights over which possum can get in the trap first.

What is the best way to clean and dye soft catch traps?

I would wire brush them clean and then dye as normal. Tests were done comparing soft catch traps to offset jaws traps. The offset traps were rated as more humane. Unless you are in a state where you have to use them, I would switch to offset jaw traps.

The size of stretchers used on muskrat seems to be the same in every state. Are there any other fur bearer sizes that remain the same regardless of the region you live in?

If you are selling to the Canadian Fur Auction, make sure your mink and beaver conform to their standards. Coon should never be wider than 8 inches at the base.

I nailed Coyote #3 on Monday. I'm going to change things up a bit today with some different smells and sets. Any thoughts would be appreciated.

Coyotes are smart and when their pals don't come back they get nervous. They don't like catch circles either. A catch circle is where a trapped animal circles the stake. Sometimes, making a new set just outside the catch circle will get you back in coyotes.

Will you please send me free snapping turtle plans?

I sell 10 homemade trap plans for $19.95. But, if you just want to trap a couple of snapping turtles, here is how. Even though there are some real monster snappers out there, some over 80 pounds, I would say the average snapper is in the 15 to 30 pound range. All you need is some 80-pound test monofilament line, some sinkers, a #2/0 hook, an 18-inch stake and a bluegill head. (Although, any kind of fish head will work.)

Take 30 feet of line, bury the hook in the fish head about 18 inches up from the hook and add a couple of sinkers. Pound the stake in the ground anywhere except in loose sand. Throw the bait out. You may have to re-bait a few times until the big snapper finds it but, this works well.

Check the set every day and re-bait as needed. Now, when you catch one, it will feel like a snag on the bottom. You have to get out in water above the turtle and pull straight up to get him off the bottom mud. Once free of the mud, you can haul him onto the shore. Grab his tail carefully, holding the head away from your body or anyone else's!! Toss him in a garbage can, cut the line, tie a new hook on, re-bait and you're back in business.

Snappers are big tough brutes and will have a nasty temper when you ruin their meal by hauling them out of the water—so be careful around them! Keep small children away. A snapper can strike about one third the length of their shell. They have a long neck. If you are ever bit by one, you'll notice they tend to hold on. If this happens, light a match and hold it under the chin until he lets your arm go.

OK Buckshot, I've gotta' hear this, how in Heaven's name do you use a Conibear to catch a fish?

It is really simple. When the fish run up to spawn in the spring, you set the shallow runs with #220's. Narrow down a spot in a stream with rocks and logs so there is just a spot wide enough for the trap. The fish have to swim up to spawn.

Could you give me the breakdown for setting snares for gray fox and red fox?

I'll do better than that. Here is the chart for setting snares for the most commonly snared animals.

	Snaring Heights	Loop Size	Preferred Cable Size	Preferred Lock
Beaver	2"	8"	3/32	Washer lock
*Bobcats	10"	12"- 14"	1/16 or 5/64	Washer lock or Camlock
Coyotes	10"	12"- 14"	3/32	Washer lock or Camlock
Gray Fox	8"	10"	5/64 or 1/16	Washer lock or Camlock
Ground Hogs	2"	6"	1/16	Washer lock
Mink	1"	3.5"	3/64	Washer lock
Opossum	3"	8"	3/32 or 5/64	Washer lock
Rabbits	2"	5"- 6"	1/16	Washer lock
Raccoon	3"	8"	3/32 or 5/64	Washer lock
*Red Fox	8"	10"	5/64 or 1/16	Washer lock
Skunk	2"	6"	1/16	Washer lock
Squirrel	1"	2.5"- 4"	3/64 or 1/16	Washer lock

*Note: If you're in Coyote country, you may want to use a cable size of 3/32.

A Word About Game Animals

I thought long and hard about writing this chapter. I was concerned that someone would go out and test this information on their own, without being in a crisis situation, "TEOTWAWKI," (The End Of The World As We Know It) or a true wilderness survival situation. I finally came to the conclusion that people need the information. After all, trapping is probably the most fundamental survival skill you can acquire which, in my opinion, obliges me to provide this information. But, I cannot be responsible for an individual's misuse of this knowledge. Think about this chapter, but please, do not try these sets unless you are in a life or death situation.

In the state of Michigan, trapping and hunting is done in the fall, with the exceptions of spring beaver trapping and spring turkey hunting. Each state has its own regulations on trapping and hunting. In the state of Michigan, for example, you can hunt some animals, but never trap them and you can trap others, but never hunt them. Other animals can be both hunted and trapped. In those cases, you can see why you should always take your gun with you when you run your traps so you can pick up tasty rabbits, grouse, squirrels and deer during the appropriate seasons. Refer to this general chart for the state of Michigan to give you an idea of the regulations that may hold true in your state. Then, before you go out, make sure you get your state's specific guidelines.

Game animals—which by Michigan's definition are those animals that are legal to hunt only—are illegal to trap or snare in almost, if not all, states. Refer to the chart on the following page to familiarize yourself with the animals that can be, or are, illegal to trap or snare in your state. Fines for snaring game animals can and do run into thousands of dollars and in some cases jail time. It is up to you to check and comply with your state's game laws. The author and the publisher will not take responsibility for your risk or actions. Enough said!!

Animal	Legal to Hunt?	Legal to Trap?	Legal to Hunt & Trap?
Squirrels	Yes	No	No
Rabbits	Yes	No	No
Ruffled Grouse	Yes	No	No
Waterfowl	Yes	No	No
Deer	Yes	No	No
Black Bear	Yes	No	No
Pheasants	Yes	No	No
Quail	Yes	No	No
Starling	Yes	Yes	Yes
Doves	Closed Season		
Muskrat	No	Yes	No
Mink	No	Yes	No
Beaver	No	Yes	No
Raccoons	Yes	Yes	Yes
Red Fox	Yes	Yes	Yes
Gray Fox	Yes	Yes	Yes
Coyotes	Yes	Yes	Yes
Bobcats	Yes	Yes	Yes
Fishers	No	Yes	No

Any animal, bird, or fish can be trapped. If I had to, I would snare deer. The Cam-Lock snare used for coyotes can be used to snare deer. Deer have established trails and all you would have to do is follow the trail until you find a tree or branches the deer are ducking under as they cross the trail. Place a snare there and wire off to the tree. Feed the snare through the swivel end around a stout tree. The snare loop should be off the ground about 14 inches at the bottom and 30 inches at the top, next to the branch. Place sticks on both sides of the trail to force the animal into the snare.

Rabbits, especially cottontail, are very easy to trap using a #110 Conibear. In brush piles or their den holes, place the #110 Conibear over the hole. Use a stabilizing stick, wire it to something solid and start catching rabbits. If there is snow on the ground, it is even easier. All you have to do is track the rabbits to their dens. Keep setting traps until dark or until you're out of traps. If you have a den hole or a good trail, you will catch rabbits.

If you're using the #110 Conibear trap, squirrels are the same way, easy. Squirrels have a genetic trait that says "explore any hole in a tree." So, all you need is a six inch stovepipe. Cut a slot for the spring and bend the pipe down so the trap sits in there tight. Place a trap in each end. Wire the pipe up in a feed tree or den tree. Wire it so it is on a branch horizontally or at a slight, no more than 30-degree, angle. Bait with peanut butter or crushed acorns in the middle.

Song birds like blackbirds, blue jays, etc are all edible and, in a survival situation, they can save your life. *WARNING: Song birds are protected by Federal Law. If you are caught trapping one, you will be subjected to a $500 fine and/or 6 months in jail.* Using a #110 Conibear, place bait, like raccoon fat, on the trigger. Pound two nails in the tree, leaving in inch exposed, on the inside jaws of the trap. Set the trap, squeeze the top together so the bottom jaws of the trap are snug against the nails and wire off to the tree. The birds will fly down and pick at the bait and the trap will fire, flattening them. I would think they would die instantly in the trap.

In the spring, when the fish come up the river to spawn, you can place your #110, #220 and #330 Conibears underwater in a deep hole against the bank. Using sticks, force the fish into the trap by forming a "V" out from the trap. The "V" has the bank on one side and the sticks on the other side. This leaves the trap in the middle. You will catch fish and snapping turtles. Make sure you wire the trap off to something solid. I have heard of an Alaskan trapper who uses #330's and wires them to trees when the salmon run. Apparently, he sets a dozen traps then runs back and forth all day hauling salmon out. He claims that for a deep river, it was faster than fishing. Think about it! Have you ever seen a huge fish run in a small stream? Now, think about where you would set #220-#330 Conibears and sharpen your fillet knife.

Ducks are incredibly easy to trap in a #220 Conibear and leg-holds. Spend a day watching ducks on a creek, a stream, a pond, marsh, etc. You will quickly see how to trap them. If they are in narrowed down spots in creeks or marshes, place a #220 Conibear so it is ⅓ in the water and ⅔ out from the top, center the trigger. Use stabilizing sticks and wire to a stake shoved or pounded deep in the mud.

To trap anything you just have to understand where they travel, narrow down their world and force them into a trap. You see, I look at life this way. In the spring, you fish, catch turtles, frogs, crawfish, etc. In the summer, you grow your garden. In the fall, you hunt and trap in order to get the meat and fur before the winter sets in. The reason you wait until fall is to give the animals time to have little ones and raise them to eating size. Then, in the deep winter, you snare and trap the predators down. This helps the game animals survive the winter in higher numbers.

Life is a balance. It is up to you to keep it that way. If you shoot a spring deer and she is pregnant, you just killed three deer, not one. If you shoot a hen duck in the spring, you just killed seven ducks, not one. On and on it goes. Use your head and think long term if you can. If you are starving, then of course, shoot or trap what you need. But after you have meat, then prepare to eat wild plants, fish, turtles, frogs, crawfish, etc.

A good trapper can wipe out animals in an area but it is wise to always leave seed. Then the area becomes a renewable resource. I always try to think long term if I can. Each fall, God provides a surplus of animals that can be trapped and hunted. Man has followed this plan for thousands of years. Use the natural cycle of life wisely and honorably to provide for yourself and your family.

When Animal Rights Become Animal Wrongs

Those who vehemently advocate animal rights believe they are doing the right thing by supporting groups like ALF (The Animal Liberation Front) and PETA (People for the Ethical Treatment of Animals). But, they are motivated more by their passion than the facts. The leaders of many of these groups exercise the rights and privileges of their position yet refrain from telling the whole story which involves animal harvesting and the carrying capacity of the land.

It is very easy to champion a loving cause like the protection of animals. And it is equally easy to rally support from the media and community at large. My point of view—the trapper's point of view—is not nearly as attractive or easy to embrace IF your work environment is not the great outdoors. Consider the following examples.

The San Francisco Chronicle reported in 1998 that wildlife biologists announced that cougars (mountain lions) were pushing the endangered Sierra Bighorn sheep to extinction and there was nothing they could do about it. Even though the solution was simple, it could not be executed because wildlife policy, like all public policies was crafted at the ballot box. Essentially, in a 1990 state ballot initiative, Proposition 117, cougars were given total protection because of perceived popular concern about the stability of their population. Naturally, they multiplied exponentially and began eating up the bighorns with abandon.

However, the scientists' proposed solution—strategic control or management of the cougar population—that would have eliminated a few of the more ravenous cougars, was not possible. The California Department of Fish and Game supports that notion and advocated a bill introduced to the state Assembly that would have allowed a limited take of lions in the Sierra region under a special research program. But the legislation died immediately after the Mountain

Lion Foundation indicated its opposition. Prop 117 allows cougars to be killed only if they threaten people, pets or livestock. Endangered species are not covered in the exemption. Do you sense a little hypocrisy here? Cougars are protected but the Sierra Bighorns (facing extinction) are not!

Bighorn expert John Wehausen, a biologist with the University of California's White Mountain Research Station, in criticizing the Mountain Lion Foundation's opposition said, "They're an animal rights group, not an environmental group. We (wildlife biologists) are concerned with habitat preservation and maintaining rich bioadversity, but they're concerned with the life of a particular animal in a particular place. They essentially reject science."

In fairness, let me present the Mountain Lion Foundation's response. Basically, their stance was that there was not a direct enough link between the mountain lion's activities and the decline of the bighorn population. Furthermore, it was suggested at the time that the Fish and Game's research and findings were suspicious. So, it doesn't matter if the bighorn problem could have been (or could be) minimized by managing the cougar population because apparently, California voters would disapprove.

Let me tell you a bit more about the coveted mountain lions. Once hunted nearly to extinction, they are on the rebound throughout the west. Consequently, there is a growing concern that the crafty cougar, aka mountain lion, puma and panther, is getting too comfortable around people who share its habitat. There have only been 10 recorded fatal attacks on people since 1890. However, five of them have been in the past 10 years. In Missoula, Montana, a six year old boy was jumped by a cougar while hiking with about three dozen other campers. In Colorado, cougars attacked three hikers in one year, including one 10 year old boy who was killed.

But what about in the East? Coyotes started migrating to Massachusetts from Northern New England about 25 years ago. Consider Wakefield, MA. The coyotes, who acquired a taste for household pets, have become so smart that they record the daily habits of homeowners so they know exactly when to strike. They can actually learn the people's schedules in residential areas. They wait until 10:00 am then move in and forage. And, because of a recent law barring leg traps, wildlife officials say they have lost their ability to effectively manage and track the coyote population.

John Benedetto, a professional trapper who has worked for the Massachusetts Division of Fisheries and Wildlife, has warned people about how smart coyotes are. "You can't wipe them out," he said. "That's one animal that will never be extinct." (Source: Associated Press; 1997) So, they can run free, without fear or apprehension of humans or their habitat, forage, devour pets, threaten people's lives and procreate (there are an estimated 4000 coyotes breeding in MA alone) with no risk of extinction. And, there's nothing that can be done about it because the voters said that leg traps are cruel.

In Asheboro, NC in 1998, a seven year old girl was attacked by a rabid fox and became the latest victim in America's worst rabies epidemic in four decades. On Jordan Lake, just west of Raleigh, a rabid beaver leapt into a boat and attacked two fishermen. These attacks contributed to North Carolina's 1997 total of 839 rabies cases; in 1990, there were only ten recorded cases. In Tennessee that same year, the rabies problem was so serious that officials were on "rabid racoon alert." In Florida, a 79 year old woman stepped outside her mobile home in Hernanado County and was attacked by a rabid red fox. She died a few months later.

Perhaps you've heard the story about Casey Read. In Pacific Grove, CA, where Casey Read lives, there is an extremely high raccoon population—an estimated 1200-2000 coons living in a one square mile area. The population grew because a large number of residents were feeding them. Casey accidentally ingested some raccoon feces which contained Baylisascaris procyonis, a raccoon roundworm. His symptoms started with irritability and slight tremors in his arm and progressed to loss of motor function, blindness and deafness. Casey Read was 13 months old and was victimized by an infection that killed at least four other children. Today, Casey is at home but is under 24 hour care. It doesn't look good for the little guy.

If you're interested in learning more or contributing to the Casey Read Fund, you may contact: Wildlife Management Services; ICO: Casey Read; 514 Equitation Lane; Felton, DE 19943.

When a county nuisance control agency was brought in to begin trapping the problem raccoons, *animal rights groups and a large number of residents protested and even held candlelight vigils in honor of the raccoons.* In thirty days, there were 45 raccoons caught in the area where Casey was believed to have been infected. Of the 150 raccoons captured throughout Pacific Grove, 100% were infected. The town was threatened with a lawsuit if trapping continued. Did you get that? The town was threatened with a lawsuit if they continued to trap out the diseased raccoons that had killed and wounded little neighborhood children. Would you sue a town for tracking down a serial killer or rapist who had victimized five children or adults? No! But don't touch the killer animals!

The extremists in the animal rights movement place animals above humans and have certainly done as much damage to our environment as they claim to have protected it. In 1998, I heard about a series of fires that were set to buildings and chair lifts to protest a plan to expand a Vail Mountain ski resort. It was done to save the lynxes but caused millions of dollars in damages. The funny part is that the Colorado Department of Fish and Game in 1998 was up in Alaska trying to catch lynxes to reintroduce them to Colorado. In short, there were no lynxes to protect in the first place.

I have heard many people say they are afraid to have their wife wear a fur coat because of the damage that could be inflicted upon her. Well, ladies put your coats back on and men put your pants back on. If someone spray painted your car because the exhaust fumes were killing animals, would you stand there and do nothing? Of course not, you would call the police and have him or her arrested for destruction of property. So, if someone should spray your fur coat, wouldn't you do the same thing? Of course! Anyone would! So, why aren't they arrested after spray painting a fur coat? The truth is these groups generally have one of their followers wear the fur coat while another one throws the paint.

That reminds me of another incident I heard about that happened about ten years ago, I believe in Indiana. A teenage boy and girl were skinny-dipping and supposedly, the boy dove in and got a muskrat leg-hold trap around his testicle. Well, they called the police and the police were suspicious right off the bat because the boy had a thumb on each side of the trap which stopped it from closing firm on his privates.

The two teenagers were separated and questioned by the police. One of the police officers knew that trapping season had been closed for five months and grew even more suspicious. The boy broke down and told the truth. He did it for his girlfriend who was a promoter of animal rights. That boy must have been in love to do something that stupid.

Every time I hear an anti-trapper spout off, I can tell within one minute if he or she has a clue about wildlife and nature. The rule is simple. You are either predator or prey. This includes humans, dogs and house cats. In the predator world, this applies every day. Man has kept people, pets and livestock safe by hunting and trapping. This teaches the other animals that we are the top predators and it is best to leave us alone. This is true for hound hunting also. The wild predators learned to fear the dogs.

Nature provides us with a surplus bounty of every animal each fall. To keep nature in balance, all we have to do is harvest the surplus. You name the animal and this applies. As Aldo Leopold stated back in the early 1900s, wildlife conservation is not *non-use*, but *wise use* of a natural resource.

There is only one way to close this discussion. I received an e-mail from a subscriber named "Outlaw" who was a bit outraged by Proposition 4 (in CA) which eliminated leg-holds, Conibears and snares, leaving cage live traps as the only legal trapping method allowed. He went on to share his opinion about the misrepresentations the animal rights activists have helped carve into accepted facts. He ended his message with the following: "P.S. Wake up sportsmen. I know you are a private, solitude, peaceful bunch, but you must unite and beware. God Bless, we need it." Enough said!!!...for the moment, anyway.

A fox with mange caught in Bridgehampton, NY. Photo courtesy of Mike Anderson.

Calf killing days are over.

Chicken killing days are over.

Recommended Reading

Each of the titles below is available from QW, Inc.—
the Distributors of Buckshot's Modern Trapper's Guide
for Xtreme Safety, Survival, Profit, Pleasure.
To place an order, or for more information, contact:

QW, Inc.
Phone:(800)838-8854; Fax:(810)954-1085
e-mail: qwinc@earthlink.net.

Mention "Buckshot" and you will receive a "Buckshot" discount!

The Official Pocket Edible Plant Survival Manual
by Robert Pelton
$15.00 (plus $4.00 post./handling)

This field guide to edible plants fits in your pocket and teaches you to identify, prepare and eat what nature provides.

Also available in the Official Pocket Survival Manual series:
The Official Pocket Survival Manual
by Robert Pelton—$15.00 (plus $4.00 post/handling)
The Official Pocket Medical Survival Manual
by Robert Pelton—$15.00 (plus $4.00 post/handling)
The Official Pocket Medicinal Plant Survival Manual
by Robert Pelton—$15.00 (plus $4.00 post/handling)

**Animal Tracks and Signs of
North America**
by Richard P. Smith
$16.95 (plus $4.00 postage/handling)

An excellent resource for learning to recognize and interpret
wildlife clues. Contains actual photos of animal and bird tracks
as they appear in the wild and gives you basic instructions
for learning tracking techniques and recognizing various
family groups.

**The Complete Book of Tanning
Skins and Furs**
by James Churchill
$18.95 (plus $4.00 postage/handling)

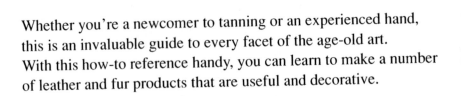

Whether you're a newcomer to tanning or an experienced hand,
this is an invaluable guide to every facet of the age-old art.
With this how-to reference handy, you can learn to make a number
of leather and fur products that are useful and decorative.

About the Author

Bruce "Buckshot" Hemming is a native of Michigan and has been trapping for 25 years. Professionally trained, Buckshot honed his trapping skills in the woods and wilds from Maine to Texas and Idaho to Indiana. He is a frequent speaker and trainer throughout North America and is renowned for his hands-on expertise.

A prolific writer and author, Buckshot is also owner/operator of Buckshot's Trapping Supplies and hosts the website www.survival-center.com/buckshot. Buckshot resides in the Upper Peninsula of Michigan with his wife Linda.

Index

A
Alligators, 148
Animal Tracks, 15, 17
Antelope, 15

B
Bank dens, 9, 44, 46, 146
Bats, 148
Bears, 4, 6, 10, 82, 164
Beavers, 5, 7–12, 14, 16–18, 22, 23,
    26–30, 33, 37, 41, 42, 50, 54–58, 60,
    70, 71, 74, 76, 85–87, 92–94, 96,
    97, 125, 126, 130, 132, 135, 136,
    138–140, 145, 146, 148, 154–159,
    161, 163, 164, 169
Bedding the trap, 62–63
Bobcats, 5, 6, 8, 10, 15–17, 21, 22, 29,
    33, 36, 69–71, 76, 78, 79, 92, 95, 128,
    154, 156, 160, 164
Body gripper, 25, 28

C
Cage traps, 25, 29, 40
Cased skinning, 92
Coil-spring, 25, 28, 30, 34, 40, 53
Conibear traps, 5, 7, 9, 11, 26, 28, 30,
    34–39, 45–50, 52–55, 57–60, 70, 71,
    75, 76, 78, 84, 88, 145–148, 155,
    157–159, 162, 164–166, 171
Cows, 11, 13, 15
Coyotes, 5, 6, 8, 15–18, 27, 28, 30, 33,
    35, 36, 45, 61–63, 67–69, 71, 75, 76,
    84–86, 92, 95, 127, 154, 156, 160,
    161, 164, 168, 169
Cubby set, 70, 76, 79

D
Dam cross-over set, 55, 60
Deep water, 26, 27, 42, 45–47, 49–51,
    53, 55–58, 158
Deer, 5, 6, 15, 30, 65, 67, 68, 70, 82–85,
    126, 130, 131, 135, 136, 156, 157,
    159, 163, 164, 166
Delta Waterfowl, 12
Dirt hole set, 62, 64, 80, 160
Distance, 16, 44, 53, 65, 76, 162
Double long-spring, 25, 27

D
Double stake swivel, 62, 78
Drowning rig, 42

E
Elk, 15, 144
Emergency tanning, 123–124
Essential traps, 30
Exclusion tube, 148

F
Farm trapping, 12, 71
Feed beds, 7, 9, 44–46
Fishers, 21, 75–78, 154, 157, 158, 164
Flat set, 62, 65, 66, 69, 71, 79, 154
Fleshing, 30, 92–94, 121
Floats, 43, 46
Footprints, 15, 157
Foxes, 6, 8, 14–19, 27, 28, 30, 33, 35,
    36, 45, 61–69, 71–73, 75, 76, 85, 92,
    95–97, 121, 127, 146, 153, 154, 156,
    160, 164, 169, 172
Freeze-proofing, 77, 152
Freshwater crawdads, 130–131
Fur bearers, 12, 14, 44, 134, 160
Fur Harvester's Auction, Inc., 91, 97
Fur prices, 96
Fur sign, 9

G
Game Animals, 6, 39, 84, 134, 163, 166
Game birds, 15, 72
Gland lures, 62, 65, 66, 79
Gray fox, 8, 18, 36, 66, 67, 127, 164
Gutting, 134

H
Hollow log set, 52, 53, 75

L
Laminating, 31
Land trapping, 7, 27, 28, 36, 61, 62, 77
Leaning pole set, 75, 76, 78
Leg-holds, 26, 27, 29, 31, 34, 36, 38, 42,
    53, 57, 60, 62, 70, 75–77, 86, 149,
    155, 166, 171
Log set, 45, 51, 52, 57, 75
Long-spring, 25–28, 35, 40, 47, 74, 157

Lures, 4, 17, 30, 43, 45, 47, 50–58, 62, 64–66, 69, 70, 72, 76, 79, 80, 131, 153–157

M

Marten, 29, 75, 157
Medium game snares, 85
Minks, 5, 8, 10, 19, 23, 27–29, 41, 42, 45, 50–54, 59, 74, 92, 95, 97, 156, 157, 159, 161, 164
Moyles Mink & Tanning, 123, 124
Mud pie set, 56
Muskrats, 3, 6–11, 14–17, 20, 23, 26–30, 33, 37, 39, 41, 42, 44–48, 50–52, 54, 74, 82, 92, 95–97, 129–132, 135, 137, 156–160, 164, 171

O

Offset jaws, 25, 31, 67, 160
Opossums, 8, 15, 20, 33, 71, 72, 93, 95
Otters, 8, 19, 29, 42, 53, 54, 59, 95, 97, 156, 157, 159

P

Packbasket, 43
Pan covers, 63–65
Patterns, 5, 7, 8, 15, 16
Pigtail supports, 85
Porcupines, 16, 130
Pres2Pur water filter, 152

R

Rabbits, 5, 6, 15, 27, 29, 30, 33, 35, 44, 67, 69, 74, 81, 82, 84, 125, 126, 130, 132, 135, 142, 163–165
Raccoons, 3, 5, 6, 11, 12, 15, 20, 28, 30, 32, 33, 37, 41, 42, 45, 48–50, 71, 72, 74, 76, 87, 92, 93, 95, 97, 130, 132, 135, 138, 148, 164, 165, 169, 170
Red fox, 17, 19, 36, 63, 66–68, 96, 97, 121, 153, 154, 164, 169

S

Scouting, 3, 4, 8–10, 43
Sheep, 15, 167
Sifter, 43, 53, 63, 64, 80
Single long-spring, 25–27
Skinning, 30, 92–94, 130, 134, 152, 153
Skunks, 15, 16, 20, 29, 71–74, 92, 93, 148, 159

Small game snares, 30, 84
Smoke tanning, 124, 126
Snapping turtle, 130, 131, 161, 165
Snares, 25, 30, 81–90, 155, 171
Snaring, 81–84, 86–88, 163
Squirrels, 5, 6, 27, 29, 30, 75, 84, 136, 142, 146–148, 157, 163–165
Stake, 31, 32, 42, 43, 45–48, 50–53, 56, 57, 62, 64, 65, 67, 71, 77, 78, 82, 83, 85, 86, 89, 149, 159, 161, 166
Steel stakes, 62, 78
Super stakes, 86
Swivels, 31, 42, 62, 63, 67, 78, 83, 85, 164

T

Tanning fur, 123

U

Urine, 17, 62, 63, 65–67, 134
Urine post set, 62, 66

W

Water trapping, 6, 7, 27, 41, 42, 58, 71
Weasels, 21, 27, 33, 51, 74, 75, 157, 158
Wedge Boards, 95
Wild plants, 132, 166
Wire carrier, 42
Wooden stretchers, 92, 94

Y

Yoho shovel, 43